CAMBRIDGE

Official Cambridge Exam Preparation

T0349645

PREPARE

WORKBOOK WITH DIGITAL PACK

Garan Holcombe   **Second Edition**

A1

LEVEL 1

Cambridge University Press
www.cambridge.org/elt

Cambridge Assessment English
www.cambridgeenglish.org

Information on this title: www.cambridge.org/9781009023016

© Cambridge University Press and Cambridge Assessment 2015, 2019, 2021

This publication is in copyright. Subject to statutory exception
and to the provisions of relevant collective licensing agreements,
no reproduction of any part may take place without the written
permission of Cambridge University Press.

First published 2015
Second Edition 2019
Second Edition update 2021

20 19 18 17 16 15 14 13 12 11 10 9

Printed in Malaysia by Vivar Printing

A catalogue record for this publication is available from the British Library

ISBN 978-1-00-902301-6 Workbook with Digital Pack
ISBN 978-1-00-902300-9 Student's Book with eBook
ISBN 978-1-00-902302-3 Teacher's Book with Digital Pack

The publishers have no responsibility for the persistence or accuracy
of URLs for external or third-party internet websites referred to in this publication,
and do not guarantee that any content on such websites is, or will remain,
accurate or appropriate. Information regarding prices, travel timetables, and other
factual information given in this work is correct at the time of first printing but
the publishers do not guarantee the accuracy of such information thereafter.

CONTENTS

IN THE CLASSROOM

VOCABULARY The alphabet

🔊 **1** Listen and choose the correct names.

01

1 (Julia) / Julie

2 Brian / Bryan

3 Tracy / Tracey

4 Steven / Stephen

5 Vicki / Vicky

6 Stewart / Stuart

Numbers

2 Circle seven numbers.

eightthree(one)sixtwentyelevenfifteenthirteen

3 Write the numbers.

			sixteen
one			seventeen
two	seven	twelve	eighteen
			nineteen
four	nine	fourteen	
five	ten		

Days

4 Write the days.

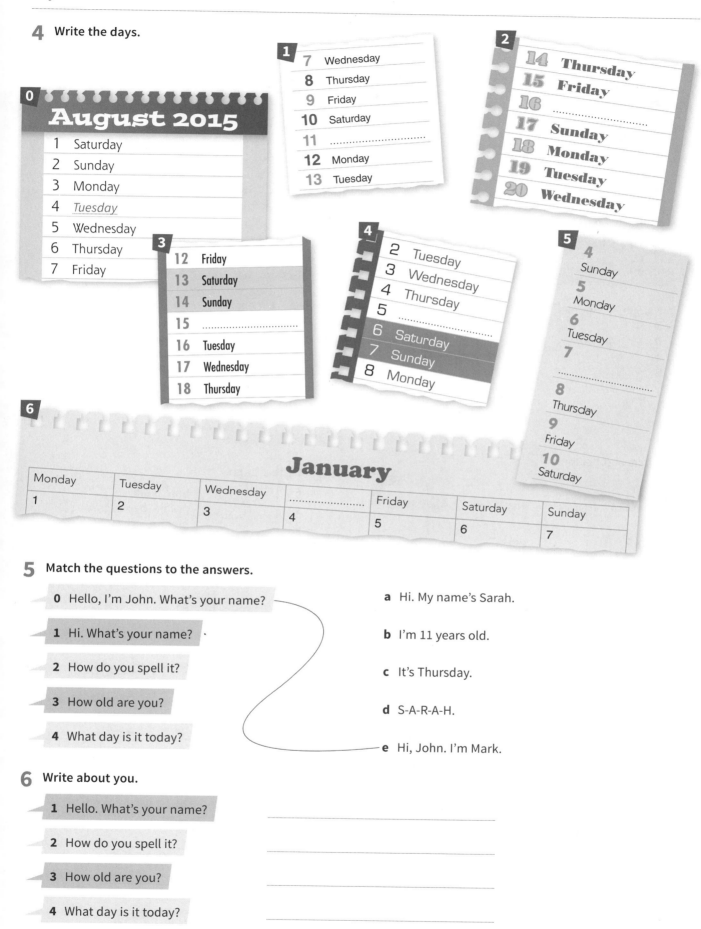

0
August 2015

1	Saturday
2	Sunday
3	Monday
4	*Tuesday*
5	Wednesday
6	Thursday
7	Friday

1
7	Wednesday
8	Thursday
9	Friday
10	Saturday
11	....
12	Monday
13	Tuesday

2
14	Thursday
15	Friday
16	....
17	Sunday
18	Monday
19	Tuesday
20	Wednesday

3
12	Friday
13	Saturday
14	Sunday
15	....
16	Tuesday
17	Wednesday
18	Thursday

4
2	Tuesday
3	Wednesday
4	Thursday
5	....
6	Saturday
7	Sunday
8	Monday

5
4	Sunday
5	Monday
6	Tuesday
7	
....	
8	Thursday
9	Friday
10	Saturday

6
January

Monday	Tuesday	Wednesday	....	Friday	Saturday	Sunday
1	2	3	4	5	6	7

5 Match the questions to the answers.

0 Hello, I'm John. What's your name?

1 Hi. What's your name?

2 How do you spell it?

3 How old are you?

4 What day is it today?

a Hi. My name's Sarah.

b I'm 11 years old.

c It's Thursday.

d S-A-R-A-H.

e Hi, John. I'm Mark.

6 Write about you.

1 Hello. What's your name? ....

2 How do you spell it? ....

3 How old are you? ....

4 What day is it today? ....

The classroom

7 Look at the picture and write the words. Use *one*, *two*, *three*, *four* and *six*.

apple	books	boys	desk	girls	orange	pen	pencils	ruler	teacher

0 _four books_   **3** _____   **6** _____   **9** _____

1 _____   **4** _____   **7** _____

2 _____   **5** _____   **8** _____

Colours

8 Circle eight colours.

Monday 5ᵗʰ September   Miss Wilson   Class 2A.

five   yellow   boy   teacher   blue   red   (orange)   pencil   six   eleven   brown   desk   green   apple   grey   black   book   white

GRAMMAR   *a / an*

1 Write *a* or *an*.

0 _a_ blue book
1 _____ orange pencil case
2 _____ picture
3 _____ green rubber
4 _____ apple
5 _____ red pen

this, that, these, those

2 Read and colour.

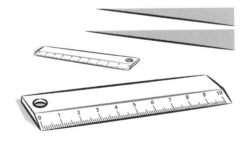

1 This ruler is orange. That ruler is green.

2 These pens are blue. Those pens are yellow.

3 Colour and write.

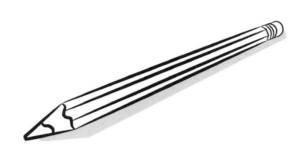

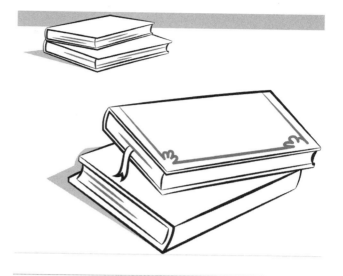

....

....

....

....

Months

1 Write the words in the right order.

April	August	~~December~~	February
~~January~~	July	June	March	May
November	October	September

1 *January*
2 ....
3 ....
4 ....
5 ....
6 ....
7 ....
8 ....
9 ....
10 ....
11 ....
12 *December*

LISTENING

🔊 02 **1** Listen and write the birthdays.

1 Lucy   *April*
2 Lee
3 Tom
4 Jane
5 Melissa
6 Oliver
7 Mia
8 Jack
9 Maria
10 William

WRITING

1 Find fourteen words. Write the words in the table.

f	o	u	r	p	e	n	g	r	e	e	n
t	e	a	c	h	e	r	a	p	r	i	l
m	o	n	d	a	y	y	e	l	l	o	w
s	e	v	e	n	j	u	n	e	r	e	d
t	h	u	r	s	d	a	y	b	o	o	k
j	a	n	u	a	r	y	e	i	g	h	t

numbers	colours	days	months	the classroom
four				

1 ALL ABOUT ME

VOCABULARY AND LISTENING

Objects and people

1 Complete the words.

0 c _a_ _m_ era
1 da _____
2 f _____ end
3 p _____ ne
4 pho _____

5 stud _____
6 w _____ ch
7 ch _____
8 b _____ g
9 t _____ le

2 Look at the pictures. Complete the sentences with words from Exercise 1.

Hi. My name's Michelle. Look at this
0 _____ _photo_ _____.
This girl is my
1 _____.
Her name's Laura.

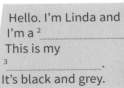 

Hello. I'm Linda and I'm a **2** _____.
This is my
3 _____.
It's black and grey.

Hi. I'm Tomas. This is my **4** _____.
It's white. This is my
5 _____.

🔊 03 3 Listen to the conversation. Is it Eve's or Joe's birthday today?

🔊 03 4 Listen again. Number the sentences in the order you hear them.

A You're in my class! ☐ 1
B See you Monday! ☐
C I'm Joe. ☐
D Today's my birthday! ☐
E I'm 12. ☐
F My name's Eve. ☐

🔊 03 5 Listen again. Are the sentences right (✓) or wrong (✗)?

0 Eve is in Joe's class. ✓
1 Joe is 12 years old. _____
2 Martha is 13 years old. _____
3 Eve is 13 years old. _____
4 Eve's phone is green and blue. _____
5 Joe's phone number is 60732982. _____

GRAMMAR   Determiners

1 Match the pronouns to the determiners.

1 I   **a** his
2 you   **b** my
3 he   **c** her
4 she   **d** your

2 Choose the correct words to complete the sentences.

0 I'm Michelle. Laura is *my* / *her* friend.
1 She's 12 today. It's *her* / *his* birthday.
2 Look at that boy. *His* / *Her* name's Tom.
3 Jon's my friend. *His* / *Your* bag's red.
4 You're a student. What's *my* / *your* name?
5 She's Azra. This is *his* / *her* watch.
6 I'm 13. This is *my* / *his* phone.
7 Amy is my sister. This is *his* / *her* camera.
8 He's my friend. *His* / *Her* name's Liam.

be singular ⊕

3 Look at the example (0). Rewrite the sentences.

0 It is my book.
It's my book.
1 I am Michelle.

2 You are my friend.

3 He is my dad.

4 She is my teacher.

5 It is blue.

6 She is my mother.

7 He is a student.

8 She is my friend.

9 I am Jack.

10 It is my phone.

4 Complete the text. Write *am* or *is*.

Pablo's blog

About me and my friends | All my posts | My favourite websites

Me

Hello! My name ⁰ _____*is*_____ Pablo and I
¹ _____ a student. I ² _____ 12 years
old. My birthday ³ _____ in December.

My friends

Javier and Laura are my friends. Javier is a
student. He's in my class. His birthday is in July.
He ⁴ _____ 12. Laura ⁵ _____
a student too. Her birthday is in January. She
⁶ _____ 13.

My teacher

My class in school is called 7A. This is Miss
Sanchez. She ⁷ _____ my teacher.

VOCABULARY AND READING

Countries and nationalities

1 Circle five nationalities.

i	t	a	l	i	a	n	s	c
t	u	r	k	i	s	h	p	h
r	u	s	s	i	a	n	a	i
g	h	f	e	t	d	l	n	n
j	z	i	a	w	r	y	i	e
m	e	x	i	c	a	n	s	s
b	v	c	u	o	r	y	h	e

2 Match the nationalities in Exercise 1 to the countries.

1 China   ....
2 Turkey   ....
3 Russia   ....
4 Spain   ....
5 Mexico   ....
6 Italy   ....

3 Complete the sentences with the correct nationality or country.

1 Augustin is from Argentina.
He's ....
2 Sara is from Spain. She's ....
3 Sergey is from ....
He's Russian.
4 Fernanda is from ....
She's Mexican.
5 Lorenzo is from ....
He's Italian.
6 Gizem is from ....
She's Turkish.
7 Lin is from China. She's ....
8 Bruno is from Brazil. He's ....

4 Read the texts. Match them to the pictures.

0 Hi! My name's Burak. I'm from Turkey and I'm 12 years old. This is a photo of me and my new school bag. I like it!

1 This is Ana. This is Maria. Ana is 11 years old. Maria is 13 years old. Ana is from Brazil and Maria is from Mexico. Ana is funny. Maria is funny too.

2 This is Iris. She's my friend. Her dad's from Spain, but she's from England. Iris is 14 years old. Her camera is new.

3 This is my friend Viktor. He's 15 years old and he's from Portugal. His mum's from Portugal too, but his dad's from Russia. His phone is nice.

4 These are my friends Luca and Marco. Luca is from Italy. Marco is from Italy too. Luca is 14 years old. Marco is 12 years old.

5 Read the text again. Complete the sentences.

1 Burak is .... years old.
2 Ana is .... years old.
3 Maria is from ....
4 Iris's .... is from Spain.
5 Iris is from ....
6 Viktor is Burak's ....
7 Viktor is .... years old.
8 Luca is from ....
9 Marco is .... years old.

be plural ➕

1 Rewrite the sentences.

0 We are from Mexico.
We're from Mexico.

1 You are from China.

2 They are from Italy.

3 We are from Brazil.

4 They are from Turkey.

5 You are from Spain.

6 We are from Russia.

7 We are from Argentina.

8 You are from Mexico.

be singular and plural ➖

2 Complete the sentences.

0 Rita is Italian. She _____isn't_____ Spanish.
1 Hello. I'm Irina. I'm from Russia.
I _____ from Brazil.
2 Elif and Emre _____ from Italy.
They're from Turkey. They're Turkish.
3 Zhang Wei is from China. He's Chinese.
He _____ Mexican.
4 Hi. I'm Ana. I'm Argentinian. I _____
from Spain.
5 Igor and Nikolai are from Russia. They
_____ from Turkey.
6 Carlos is Spanish. He _____ Italian.
7 Chiara and Martina are from Italy. They
_____ from Argentina.
8 Manuela is Mexican. She _____
Brazilian.

3 Read the sentences. Write negative sentences.

0 She's Turkish.
She isn't / is not Turkish.

1 He's Spanish.

2 She's from China.

3 You're Mexican.

4 They're from Brazil.

5 I'm from Italy.

6 She's Argentinian.

1 Read the description. Answer the questions.

Hi! My name's Claudia. I'm 13 years old. I'm from Italy. I'm Italian. These are my parents. They aren't from Italy. They're from Argentina. They're Argentinian.

1 What is her name?

2 How old is she?

3 Where is she from?

4 What nationality is she?

5 Where are her parents from?

6 Where nationality are they?

2 Write about you.

1 Hello, I'm Martin. What's your name?

2 I'm 11 years old. How old are you?

3 I'm from Brazil. Where are you from?

4 I'm Brazilian. What nationality are you?

5 My parents are from Mexico. Where are your parents from?

6 Goodbye.

2 MY FAMILY

Families

1 Look at the pictures. Complete the table with the words in the box.

> baby   ~~child~~   brother   children   dad
> ~~daughter~~   father   husband   mother
> mum   parents   sister   ~~son~~   wife

daughter	*son*	*child*

2 Write the word. Use words from Exercise 1.

0 *parents* and children
1 son and
2 and wife
3 brother and
4 mother and
5 and dad

3 Write about your family.

Susan is my mother. Michael is my father.

4 Read the email. What nationality is Selen?

5 Read again. Match the names to the family words.

1 Azra   **a** mother
2 Ali   **b** sister
3 Hasan   **c** father
4 Dilan   **d** brother

6 Read again. Are the sentences right (✓) or wrong (✗)?

1 Olga is 15.
2 Olga is from Russia.
3 Selen is from Izmir.
4 Selen is 14 years old.
5 Azra is five years old.
6 Hasan is very funny.

Hi Olga,

Thank you very much for your email and the photos of your family and of your country, Russia. How old is your sister?

I'm 13 years old too! Look at my photo – this is me with my new phone!

This is a photo of my family. My family is Turkish. We're from a place called Izmir. Izmir is in Turkey.

My mum's name is Dilan and my father's name is Ali. My sister is called Azra. She is 11 years old. Our brother is five years old. His name's Hasan. He is a very funny boy!

Love from,

Selen

Possessive 's

1 Look at the picture. Complete the sentences. Write *Billy's* or *Laura's*.

0 Liam is _____*Laura's*_____ son.
1 Liam is _____ brother.
2 Holly is _____ sister.
3 Holly is _____ daughter.
4 Nick is _____ husband.
5 Nick is _____ father.

Hello. I'm Liam. This is my family.

Nick
Laura
Billy
Liam
Holly

Determiners

2 Complete the table.

pronoun	determiner
I	1
you	2
he	3
she	4
we	5
they	6

3 Choose the correct words to complete the sentences.

0 I'm Liam and Holly is (my)/ your sister.

1 Laura and Nick are *our* / *their* parents.

2 Laura is *our* / *their* mum.

3 Nick is *our* / *their* dad.

4 We're *our* / *their* children.

5 I'm *our* / *their* son.

6 Holly is *our* / *their* daughter.

4 Complete the text with *our* or *their*.

Families around the world:
Mexico

My name is Luis and this is my sister Mariana. We are from Mexico. This is ⁰ _____*our*_____ family. ¹_____ parents are Sandra and Esteban. Sandra is ² _____ mum. Esteban is ³ _____ dad. We're ⁴ _____ children. I'm ⁵ _____ son. Mariana is ⁶ _____ daughter.

Adjectives: feelings

1 Put the letters in the right order to make adjectives.

0 t h o   *hot*
1 s d a
2 c e i n
3 e r t d i
4 d b e o r
5 e e v c l r
6 p a y p h
7 y u r n h g
8 n u n y f

2 Complete the sentences. Use the words from Exercise 1.

1 I'm _____ .

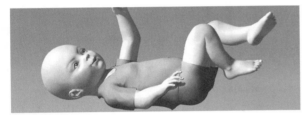

2 Our baby sister's _____ .

18 x 17 = 306

3 Your friend's _____ .

4 Your teacher's _____ .

5 Your dad's _____ .

6 I'm _____ .

7 You and your friends are _____ .

8 We're _____ .

9 Your sister's _____ .

3 Listen to the conversation. Where is Anna from?

4 Listen to the conversation again. Choose the right sentence (✓).

0 **A** Anna is Alex's friend. ✓
  B Anna is Alex's mum. ☐

1 **A** Anna's family is from England. ☐
  B Anna's family is from Russia. ☐

2 **A** Alex's mum is from Russia. ☐
  B Alex's dad is from Russia. ☐

3 **A** Alex and Anna are hungry. ☐
  B Alex and Anna aren't hungry. ☐

4 **A** The film is sad. ☐
  B The film isn't sad. ☐

1 Complete the questions with *Is* or *Are*.

1 _____ you Chinese?
2 _____ your parents Russian?
3 _____ it Monday?
4 _____ you tired?
5 _____ your English teacher clever?
6 _____ you hungry?
7 _____ your friend funny?
8 _____ you bored?

2 Answer the questions in Exercise 1 so they are true for you.

1 _____
2 _____
3 _____
4 _____
5 _____
6 _____
7 _____
8 _____

3 Read the sentences. Write the questions and short answers.

0 I'm tired.
Are you tired?
Yes, I am.
1 Sophie is happy.
_____
2 James isn't bored.
_____
3 My friends aren't hungry.
_____
4 Our classroom isn't hot.
_____
5 My sister is funny.
_____
6 My mum is clever.
_____

4 Put the words in the right order to make questions.

0 your / What / name / is ?
What is your name?
1 from / are / Where / you ?
_____
2 is / birthday / your / When ?
_____
3 number / What / your / is / phone?
_____
4 friends / Where / your / are ?
_____

1 Correct the sentences with capital letters.

0 my friend is called Vladimir
My friend is called Vladimir.
1 vladimir's from russia
_____
2 he's russian
_____
3 he's 14 years old
_____
4 today he's tired!
_____

2 Read the description. Complete the table.

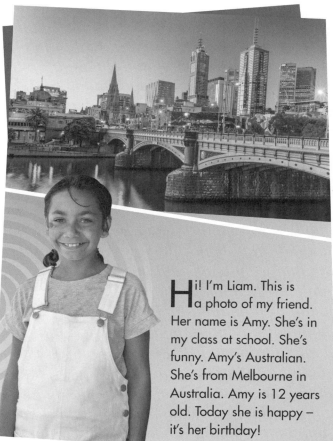

Hi! I'm Liam. This is a photo of my friend. Her name is Amy. She's in my class at school. She's funny. Amy's Australian. She's from Melbourne in Australia. Amy is 12 years old. Today she is happy – it's her birthday!

name	1 _____
age	2 _____
nationality	3 _____
today she is …	4 _____

3 Write about your friend. Remember to use capital letters and full stops.

My name is _____ .
My friend's name is _____ .
He/She is _____ years old.
He's _____ .
He/She is from _____ .
Today he/she is _____ .

3 MY HOME

VOCABULARY AND LISTENING

Rooms

1 Circle 12 house words.

l	i	v	i	n	g	r	o	o	m
b	e	d	r	o	o	m	w	d	h
k	i	t	c	h	e	n	a	o	a
t	q	b	l	b	z	c	l	o	l
s	h	o	w	e	r	q	l	r	l
t	o	i	l	e	t	b	a	t	h
w	i	n	d	o	w	z	a	x	l
d	i	n	i	n	g	r	o	o	m
b	r	u	f	l	o	o	r	i	l
x	b	a	t	h	r	o	o	m	f

2 Complete the table. Use words from Exercise 1.

rooms	things
living room	

3 Write the house words under the pictures.

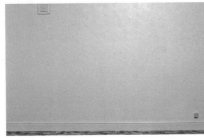

1 _____

2 _____

3 _____

4 _____

5 _____

6 _____

4 Listen to Lily describe her house. How many bedrooms are there?

5 Listen again. Tick (✓) the rooms and things Lily talks about.

0	living room	✓	**6**	bathroom	☐
1	window	☐	**7**	shower	☐
2	walls	☐	**8**	bath	☐
3	kitchen	☐	**9**	bedroom	☐
4	door	☐	**10**	hall	☐
5	dining room	☐	**11**	floor	☐

6 Listen again. Match the people to the rooms.

1 Beth   a bedroom
2 Dad   b living room
3 Mum   c dining room
4 Tom   d hall
5 Ellie   e kitchen

there is / there are; in / on

1 Put the words in the right order to make sentences.

1 is / wall / picture / There / a / the / on

2 bookcase / bag / is / There / a / on / the

3 windows / There / in / are / room / two / the

4 the / bed / in / a / room / is / There

5 two / kitchen / the / There / boys / in / are

6 girl / the / room / is / living / There / a / in

7 house / six / are / There / the / in / rooms

2 Match the words to make two sentences.

0	There's There are	seven rooms a pencil case	on in	the house. the table.
1	There's There are	six books a bath	on in	the bathroom. the floor.
2	There's There are	a boy five pictures	on in	the bedroom. the wall.
3	There's There are	three photos a baby	on in	the bath. the wall.
4	There's There are	two windows a camera	on in	the floor. the kitchen.
5	There's There are	a pet fish four girls	on in	the living room. the bookcase.

3 Complete the sentences with *There's* or *There are* and *in* or *on*.

0 *There are* two girls *in* the bedroom.

1 _____ a clock _____ the kitchen.

2 _____ two doors _____ the living room.

3 _____ a picture _____ the wall.

4 _____ three windows _____ bathroom.

5 _____ two beds _____ the bedroom.

6 _____ a bag _____ the floor.

7 _____ three boys _____ the living room.

8 _____ a book _____ the table.

9 _____ a camera _____ the table.

10 _____ board games _____ the dining room.

4 Look at the pictures. Write sentences. Use *There is / There are* and the words in the box.

door	~~girls~~	pictures	window

0 *There are two girls in the kitchen.*
1 _____
2 _____
3 _____

bed	boys	pictures	window

4 _____
5 _____
6 _____
7 _____

boy	door	girls	TV

8 _____
9 _____
10 _____
11 _____

VOCABULARY AND READING

Things in my room

1 Put the letters in the right order to make words.

- **0** e d b   *bed*
- **1** s y t o
- **2** v o n i t e e l i s
- **3** o l c c k
- **4** r e t p s o
- **5** l c s t e h o
- **6** i r u g t a
- **7** e o k a o b c s
- **8** t p e s i f h
- **9** p u c m t r o e
- **10** r a d b o g e m a

2 Look at the picture. Write *Yes* or *No*.

- **1** There are toys on the floor.
- **2** The clock is on the bookcase.
- **3** The posters are on the wall.
- **4** The computer is on the chair.
- **5** The guitar is on the bed.
- **6** There are clothes on the chair.
- **7** There is a pet fish on the desk.
- **8** There is a TV in the room.

3 Read the three descriptions. Who is from England?

Frank's room

Hi! My name's Frank. I live in Paris. Paris is in France. I'm 13 years old and I like my bedroom. I've got a bed, a desk, a chair and two big windows in my room. And I've got 12 posters on the walls! 'No more posters!' Mum says. My favourite colour is red, but the walls in my room are blue.

Luke's room

Hello. I'm Luke and I'm 11 years old. I'm from Warwick in England. My bedroom is great! The walls are yellow and blue – these are my favourite colours! On my walls I've got some posters and a nice black clock. I've got a desk in my room. There are lots of books on it!

Alex's room

Hi. My name's Alex. I'm 12 years old. I'm from Ireland, but my parents are from Scotland. My bedroom is my favourite place. I've got my clothes, my board games and my books in my room, but my favourite thing in my bedroom is my guitar – it's new! There's a computer in my room too. My friends like it!

4 Read the text again. Answer the questions.

- **0** Where is Frank from?
  He's from France.
- **1** How old is Frank?

- **2** What is Frank's favourite colour?

- **3** How old is Luke?

- **4** What are Luke's favourite colours?

- **5** Where are Luke's books?

- **6** How old is Alex?

- **7** Where is Alex from?

- **8** What is Alex's favourite thing?

have got ●

1 Put the words in the right order to make sentences.

0 got / computers / Mum's / two
Mum's got two computers.

1 got / I've / books / five

2 a / sister's / pet / My / got / fish

3 camera / a / got / Dad's

4 new / got / brother's / TV / My / a

5 four / house / bedrooms / got / has / Our

6 board game / great / We've / a / got

7 a / got / Mum's / phone / blue

8 nice / a / I've / bookcase / got

2 Match the sentences.

1 My name's Elen.
2 My sister's name is Katrina.
3 I'm Jack and my friend is George.
4 José and Juan are my friends.
5 My brother's name is Sam.

a We've got board games and toys.
b I've got a phone and a computer.
c He's got a clock and a camera.
d She's got lots of posters and two guitars.
e They've got a pet fish and a television.

3 Complete the sentences with *'s got* or *'ve got*.

0 I'm Luisa. It's my birthday today.
I *'ve got* a new camera.
1 Mateo's my friend. He _____
two brothers and three sisters.
2 Tom and Amanda _____
three children.
3 We're Harry and Jacob. We
_____ three pet fish in our
living room.
4 My sister _____ lots of
books in her room.
5 Amelia and Poppy _____
lots of friends. They are happy.
6 Helen and Richard are my parents. They
_____ a TV in their
bedroom.
7 You're a student. You _____
ten books and a computer on your desk.
8 My brother _____ a new
bag for school. It's red and black.

1 Read the text. Choose the correct words.

My home

This is my family and this is ⁰ our / *their*
home. We live in a new flat. I like our flat.
It's a ¹ *tired* / *happy* place.

In the flat there ² *are* / *is* four bedrooms.
³ *We've* / *She's* also got a kitchen, a bathroom,
a living room and a dining room. Oh, and a
hall too!

My favourite room is ⁴ *his* / *my* bedroom!
I've got pictures on the walls and lots of
board games. In my bedroom, I've also got
a computer, a TV and a guitar.

2 Write about your home and your bedroom.
Use the text in Exercise 1 to help you.

- I live in a _____.
- There are _____
  bedrooms.
- We've also got _____
- My favourite room is _____.
- In my bedroom I've got _____.

4 MY THINGS

VOCABULARY AND READING

Things in my school bag

1 Match the words in the box to the photos.

banana	chocolate	coat
football	gloves	hat	keys
scarf	wallet	water bottle

1

6

2

7

3

8

4

9

5

10

2 Read the descriptions. What type of room do the students describe?

Tell us about ...

Petra, 13, Russia
It's a very big room – there are 30 students in it! It's got a red door, light blue walls and four windows. It's got lots of small brown desks. On my desk I've got my pens, my books and a water bottle. I like my desk.

Dao, 12, Vietnam
It's a small room. There are bookcases – two, three, four! On the bookcases there are lots of English books. The room's got five small windows and a dark green door. The walls are light green. There are two long desks in the room. My bag is under the desk. In the bag, I've got my scarf and wallet.

Chiara, 11, Italy
It's a nice big room. The walls are white and there's a blue door. Oh, we've got one very big window in the room – we like it! We've got our pens and rulers on our desks, but our water bottles are in our bags.

Callum 13, England
It's a small room, but it's nice. It's got three big windows. The walls and door are yellow – it's a happy colour. There are lots of desks in the room. On my desk I've got all my pens. My bag is on the floor next to the desk. I've got my books, some chocolate and a banana in my bag.

3 Read the descriptions in Exercise 2 again. Complete the table.

	big/small	door	walls	windows
Petra's room		red		
Dao's room			light green	
Chiara's room	big			
Callum's room				three

4 Read the descriptions again. Complete the sentences.

1 Petra's room is very _____ .
2 Petra's room has got lots of _____ desks.
3 There are English _____ in Dao's room.
4 The windows in Dao's room aren't _____ .
5 Chiara's _____ is in her bag.
6 There are _____ on Callum's desk.

1 **Write the negative sentences.**

0 Miguel's got his wallet.
Miguel hasn't got his wallet.

1 Irene's got her football.

2 Dad's got his water bottle.

3 I've got my blue bag.

4 Emilio's got his red hat.

5 Mum's got her long scarf.

6 Sara's got her black gloves.

7 Charlotte's got her white guitar.

8 Marco's got his watch.

9 I've got my red coat.

10 Jess's got her new phone.

2 **Look at the things in Jim's bag. Tick (✓) the right sentence.**

0 A He's got a ball. ✓
 B He's hasn't got a ball. ☐

1 A He's got his keys. ☐
 B He's hasn't got his keys. ☐

2 A He's got a coat. ☐
 B He hasn't got a coat. ☐

3 A He's got a camera. ☐
 B He hasn't got a camera. ☐

4 A He's got a drink. ☐
 B He hasn't got a drink. ☐

5 A He's got a banana. ☐
 B He hasn't got a banana. ☐

3 **Complete the dialogues with *'s got / 've got* or *hasn't got / haven't got*.**

Ben: Mum, where's my football?
Mum: Ella ⁰*'s got* _____ it! She's in the garden.
Ben: Thanks, Mum.
Ben: Oh, no!
Dad: Are you OK, Ben?
Ben: No, I'm not. I ¹_____ my phone. Oh, where is it?
Dad: Your phone? Look – it's on the table!
Ben: Oh, yes! Thanks, Dad.

Ben: Dad, is my hat in Adam's bag?
Dad: Adam ²_____ your hat, Ben! Your hat's on the floor in the living room.
Ella: Ben?
Ben: Yes, Ella.
Ella: Where's my chocolate?
Ben: I ³_____ it, Ella. Is it in your bag?
Ella: What's that in your coat, Ben? Mum! Ben ⁴_____ my chocolate!
Mum: Ready, Ben?
Ben: Yes, I ⁵_____ a water bottle, some chocolate, a banana and my coat.
Mum: Your gloves and scarf?
Ben: Yes! I've got my gloves and … oh, no! I ⁶_____ my scarf! Where is it?
Mum: It's on your bed, Ben!

4 **Write about you and your family. Use *hasn't got* or *haven't got*.**

I haven't got a guitar. My sister hasn't got a camera.

VOCABULARY AND LISTENING

Adjectives: things

1 Complete the table with the adjectives from the box.

light	long	~~new~~	dirty	small

old	**0**	*new*
clean	**1**	
short	**2**	
big	**3**	
dark grey	**4**	grey

2 Look at the pictures. Complete the sentences with adjectives from Exercise 1.

1 Jessica's got a _____ scarf.
2 Sam's got a _____ bag.
3 Isabella's got a _____ grey hat.
4 Dylan and James have got a _____ football.
5 Dan's got a _____ book.
6 Ava's got a _____ guitar.

3 Look at the picture. Circle the correct adjectives.

1 I've got a/an *old* / *new* hat.
2 I've got a *long* / *short* scarf.
3 I've got a *big* / *small* book.
4 I've got a *dirty* / *clean* coat.
5 I've got a *light grey* / *dark grey* bag.

4 🔊 06 Listen to the conversation. Where is Emily?

5 🔊 06 Listen again. Are the sentences right (✓) or wrong (✗)?

0 Emily isn't tired today. _____ ✗
1 Emily's ruler is on the table. _____
2 Emily's dad has got her pens and pencils. _____
3 The maths book is on the bookcase. _____
4 Emily's coat is on the chair. _____
5 Emily's dad has got her bag. _____

6 🔊 06 Listen again. Tick (✓) the items Emily takes to school.

1 scarf ☐
2 hat ☐
3 ruler ☐
4 pens ☐
5 pencils ☐
6 water bottle ☐
7 maths book ☐
8 coat ☐

1 Answer the questions. Write short answers.

0 Has your mum got a short coat? ✓
Yes, she has.

1 Has your brother got a big bedroom? ✗

2 Have you got two pet fish? ✗

3 Have you got nice teachers? ✓

4 Have your friends got a ball? ✓

5 Has your dad got a guitar? ✗

6 Have you got a new phone? ✓

2 Write the questions. Then complete the answers.

0 A: you / hat?
Have you got a big, blue hat?
B: No, *I haven't.*

1 A: your friend / a green coat?

B: Yes, she _____ .

2 A: you / small classroom at school?

B: No, we _____ .

3 A: Tomás and Santiago / a new baby brother?

B: Yes, _____ .

4 A: your mum / dark blue bag?

B: No, _____ .

5 A: your brother / football?

B: Yes, _____ .

6 A: you / blue pencil?

B: Yes, _____ .

7 A: your parents / big bedroom?

B: No, _____ .

8 A: your sister / old computer?

B: Yes, _____ .

9 A: Holly / red scarf?

B: No, she _____ .

10 A: your friend / black guitar?
B: Yes, she _____ .

11 A: Sam / English books?
B: Yes, he _____ .

12 A: your brother / blue coat?
B: No, _____ .

1 Complete the questions in the questionnaire. Use *have got / has got*.

The family and things survey

1 _____ you got a brother or sister?

2 _____ your family got a house or a flat?

3 _____ your mum or dad got a computer?

4 _____ you got a guitar?

5 _____ you got any English books?

2 Match Jake's answers to the questions in Exercise 1.

a Yes, I have. I've got the Harry Potter books.
b I haven't got a brother, but I've got two sisters.
c No, I haven't.
d We've got a small flat. It's great.
e My mum and dad have got a new one. It's got two computer games.

3 Write about Jake.

Jake's got two sisters. He hasn't got …

4 Write your answers to the questions in Exercise 1.

1 _____
2 _____
3 _____
4 _____
5 _____

5 WHAT CAN YOU DO?

VOCABULARY AND LISTENING

Activities and skills

1 Match the words.

1 swim		**a**	phone numbers
2 sail		**b**	songs
3 cook		**c**	underwater
4 remember		**d**	English
5 play		**e**	the guitar
6 ride		**f**	skate
7 paint		**g**	a horse
8 speak		**h**	a picture
9 ice		**i**	spaghetti
10 sing		**j**	a boat

2 Write the phrases from Exercise 1.

1 _____

6 _____

2 _____

7 _____

3 _____

8 _____

4 _____

9 _____

5 _____

10 _____

◁)) **3** Listen to the conversation. What
07   quiz do they do?

◁)) **4** Listen again. Choose the right (✓)
07   sentence.

0 A Ella can ride a horse.   ☑
   B Luca can ride a horse.   ☐

1 A Ella can speak French.   ☐
   B Luca can speak French.   ☐

2 A Ella can't sing.   ☐
   B Luca can sing.   ☐

3 A Ella can cook spaghetti.   ☐
   B Luca can't cook spaghetti.   ☐

4 A Ella can swim underwater.   ☐
   B Luca can't swim underwater.   ☐

◁)) **5** Listen again. Write *Ella* or *Luca*.
07

0 _____*Ella*_____ has got a horse.
1 _____ 's mum is from
   Italy.
2 _____ 's spaghetti is very
   nice.
3 _____ can't ice skate.
4 _____ can't remember
   phone numbers.

GRAMMAR · can / can't

1 Look at the pictures. Choose the correct words.

1 Pedro and Mateo *can / can't* swim underwater.

2 Carla's mum *can / can't* sing.

3 Josh *can / can't* ride a horse.

4 Lily *can / can't* paint a picture.

5 Cameron's dad *can / can't* play the guitar.

6 Sophie's friends *can / can't* speak English.

2 Write questions. Then complete the answers.

0 you / speak English?
A: *Can you speak English?*
B: Yes, *I can* .

1 Beatriz and Jon / play the guitar?
A: _____
B: No, _____ .

2 Isabelle / ride a horse?
A: _____
B: Yes, _____ .

3 Mustafa / swim underwater?
A: _____
B: No, _____ .

4 your baby sister / paint a picture?
A: _____
B: No, _____ .

5 your friends / sing?
A: _____
B: Yes, _____ .

6 your brother / take photos?
A: _____
B: Yes, _____ .

7 your mother / ice skate?
A: _____
B: No, _____ .

8 your dad / sail a boat?
A: _____
B: No, _____ .

3 Look at the table. Write sentences using *and*, *but* and *or*. Write two sentences about each person.

	play the guitar	speak chinese	remember names	ride a horse
Merve	✗	✗	✓	✓
Juan	✗	✓	✗	✗
Amelia	✓	✗	✗	✓

0 *Merve can't play the guitar or speak Chinese.*
1 _____
2 _____
3 _____
4 _____
5 _____

WHAT CAN YOU DO? 25

Parts of the body

1 Find 11 words for parts of the body.

e	x	e	a	l	m	p	b	h
y	a	e	a	r	h	e	g	e
e	m	k	c	b	a	z	t	a
n	o	a	r	m	n	t	f	d
o	u	y	h	k	d	v	o	h
s	t	f	a	c	e	o	o	p
e	h	t	o	o	t	h	t	t
m	t	q	a	s	v	c	e	z
e	h	a	i	r	l	e	g	t

2 Write the words from Exercise 1 in the table.

	body	
eye		*arm*

3 Read the email and look at the pictures. Write the names under the right picture.

| Julia | Lisbeth | Lola | Melanie |

1 _____

2 _____   3 _____

4 _____

4 Read the email again. Complete the sentences.

0 Paola's sister can speak ___*Chinese*___ .
1 Melanie is Julia's _____ .
2 Lola is Julia's _____ .
3 Lisbeth is Julia's _____ .
4 Lisbeth has got a new _____ .
5 Julia has got a new _____ .

5 Read the email again. Are the sentences right (✓) or wrong (✗)?

1 Paola's sister is 12.   ✓
2 Julia's sister is 13.   ___
3 Lisbeth can't sing.   ___
4 Melanie can stand on one leg for a long time.   ___
5 Julia can't paint.   ___
6 Julia can't take photos.   ___

Hi Paola,

How are you? Thanks for your email. Thanks for the photos too! Can your sister really speak Chinese? And she's only 12! Wow!

Here are some photos for you. There's a photo of my sister. She's 13 years old. Her name's Lisbeth. She's got a new guitar. She can play the guitar, but she can't sing.

There's a photo of my friend, Melanie, too. She can stand on one leg for a long, long time! I think she's very funny! Can you stand on one leg for a long time, Paola? I can't, but I can take photos! There's a photo of me with my new camera.

I can paint too. Here's one of my favourite paintings. It's a painting of my cat. She's under the chair in our living room. Her name's Lola. Have you got a cat, Paola?

Can you send me more photos of your family and friends?

Love from,
Julia

1 Complete the sentences with the words in the box.

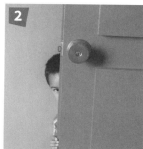

in	under	on	behind

1 The pencils are _____ the pencil case.
2 He's _____ the door.
3 The book is _____ the chair.
4 The girl is _____ the bed.

2 Complete the description. Use *in, on, under* or *behind*.

Hi! My name's Arthur and I am ⁰ _____*in*_____
my room. The desk is ¹ _____ the
chair. My guitar is ² _____ my bed.
My clock is ³ _____ the wall. My desk is
⁴ _____ the clock. There are books
⁵ _____ my bed and ⁶ _____
my desk. My laptop is ⁷ _____ my desk.
This is my favourite room ⁸ _____
my house!

3 Describe your room. Use *in, on, under* or *behind*.

My bed is under the window.
_____
_____

WRITING

1 Read the text. Write *Yes, he can* or *No, he can't.*

Hi, My name's Henry. I can't speak Spanish, but I can speak Russian. I can speak English too! I can swim underwater and I can stand on my head – but only for one minute. I can't put my hair behind my ear – my hair is very short! I can't play the guitar with my feet, but I can ice skate. What about you? What can *you* do?

0 Can Henry speak Spanish?
No, he can't.
1 Can he speak English?
_____
2 Can he swim underwater?
_____
3 Can he stand on his head for five minutes?
_____
4 Can he ice skate?
_____

2 Answer the questions in the questionnaire. Write *Yes, I can* or *No, I can't.*

CAN YOU?

1 Can you speak Russian or Spanish?
_____
2 Can you swim underwater?
_____
3 Can you stand on your head?
_____
4 Can you put your hair behind your ear?
_____
5 Can you write with your feet?
_____
6 Can you ice skate?
_____

3 Write about what you can do. Use the text in Exercise 1 and your answers in Exercise 2 to help you.

Hi, my name's …
_____
_____
_____

6 PARTY TIME!

VOCABULARY AND LISTENING

Food and drinks

1 Complete the food words.

1 _____ ce
2 m _____ k
3 jui _____
4 _____ sta

5 ca _____ s
6 _____ ips
7 s _____ p
8 br _____ d

9 butt _____
10 che _____
11 _____ cken
12 _____ cuits

13 po _____ oes
14 tomat _____
15 l _____ ade
16 e _____ g _____

2 Look at the photos. Complete the sentences with the words in the box.

bread   cake   chips   eggs   juice   pasta   rice   milk   soup   tomatoes

1 Are there any _____?

2 Is that _____?

3 Is there any _____ in the fridge?

4 We haven't got any pasta or _____.

5 Are you hungry? I've got some _____.

6 There's some _____ in the kitchen.

7 Have we got any lemonade or _____?

8 Where are the _____?

9 Have we got any _____?

3 Listen to the conversation. Why have they got a shopping list?

4 Listen again. Complete Jenny's shopping list.

Mum's party shopping list
0 _____bread_____   4 _____
1 _____   5 _____
2 _____   6 _____
3 _____

5 Listen again. Who says the sentences and questions? Write *J* for Jenny and *D* for Dad.

0 Where are you?   *D*
1 Have you got the shopping list?   _____
2 We can write a new shopping list.   _____
3 Have we got any fruit?   _____
4 We need a cake.   _____
5 Yes, that's everything.   _____
6 Where are my keys?   _____

Countable and uncountable nouns

1 Look at the words. Complete the table.

| ~~potatoes~~ | biscuits | cakes | chicken |
| rice | pasta | tomatoes | apple juice |

countable	uncountable
potatoes	

some, any, lots of

2 Look at Leo's shopping and read the sentences. Write _Yes_ or _No_.

0 He hasn't got any biscuits.
No. He's got some biscuits.

1 He's got some potatoes.

2 He's got some eggs.

3 He's got lots of bananas.

4 He's got some oranges.

5 He's got a tomato.

3 Look at Sam and Holly's shopping. Complete the sentences with _any_ and _some_.

1 They've got _____ butter.
2 They've got _____ cheese.
3 They haven't got _____ eggs.
4 They haven't got _____ tomatoes.
5 They've got _____ biscuits.
6 They haven't got _____ orange juice.
7 They haven't got _____ milk.

4 Complete the sentences with _a_, _an_, _any_, and _some_.

1 We've got _____ cheese for the party.
2 Mum, have we got _____ chocolate?
3 I've got _____ apple.
4 Dad, I haven't got _____ eggs for the cake!
5 They've got _____ nice chocolate biscuits.
6 Can I have _____ biscuit, please?

5 Read the descriptions. Match the descriptions to the pictures.

What's on your table?

A   C

B   D

1 _____
On our table there's ^{0} _some_ cheese and ^{1} _____ meat. There's also ^{2} _____ bread, but there isn't ^{3} _____ fruit. There are lots of cakes and a jug of milk, too.

2 _____
We've got ^{4} _____ eggs, bread, and butter on our table. We've got ^{5} _____ milk too. We haven't got ^{6} _____ meat.

3 _____
There are ^{7} _____ eggs on our table. There's ^{8} _____ meat too. We've also got ^{9} _____ cheese and bread. There aren't ^{10} _____ apples or bananas.

4 _____
We've got a big cake and lots of biscuits. We haven't got ^{11} _____ eggs, but we've got ^{12} _____ bread and cheese. We've got ^{13} _____ apples, too.

6 Read the descriptions again. Complete the descriptions with _some_ or _any_.

Telling the time (1)

1 Look at the clocks. Complete the sentences with words in the box.

0  10:00

1  03:10

2  18:15

3  16:00

4  19:30

5  14:15

6  08:20

7  09:00

eight	four	nine	seven
six	~~ten~~	three	two

0 It's _____ten_____ am.
1 It's _____ ten.
2 It's _____ fifteen.
3 It's _____ o'clock.
4 It's _____ thirty.
5 It's _____ fifteen.
6 It's _____ twenty.
7 It's _____ o'clock.

2 Look at the clocks. Write the times.

 17:10

 14:00

0 *It's five ten.*

3 _____

 01:00

 13:15

1 _____

4 _____

 12:30

 04:00

2 _____

5 _____

3 Read the invitations. Choose the right (✓) sentence.

1

Can you come to my party?
It's at Callie's house on Friday 28th October, from 7 until late!
Be ready for music and dancing!
CALL 0213 445 6721
Email: callie2001@greatmail.com

2

WOULD YOU LIKE TO COME BEN'S FILM PARTY?

When is it?	Saturday, 21st November
Where is it?	Ben's house
What time is it?	6 pm until 11 pm
Who can I call?	Ben on 0721 665 992

3

Carmen invites you to her party in the park!
PARTY FOOD! MUSIC! FUN!

Place	Scotland Park
Date	18th April
Time	from 12 until 4
Call	0242 766 991

4

COME TO MY COOL POOL PARTY!

WHERE	Central Swimming Pool (behind the park)
WHEN	Sunday, 10th May
TIME	From 12.00 to 3.00
FROM	Gregor
PHONE No:	0271 887 331

0 A There is music at Callie's party. ✓
   B There isn't any music at Callie party. ☐

1 A Callie's party is at her friend's house. ☐
   B Callie's party is at her house. ☐

2 A There isn't a film at Ben's. ☐
   B There is a film at Ben's party. ☐

3 A You can call Ben. ☐
   B You can't call Ben. ☐

4 A There is food at Carmen's party. ☐
   B There isn't any food at Carmen's party. ☐

5 A Carmen's party is in a house. ☐
   B Carmen's party isn't in a house. ☐

6 A Gregor's party is in the park. ☐
   B Gregor's party isn't in the park. ☐

7 A Gregor's party is on Saturday. ☐
   B Gregor's party isn't on Saturday. ☐

1 Choose the correct words to complete the sentences.

1 The party's *at / on* my house.
2 It's *at / on* 1st June.
3 It's *on / until* Friday.
4 It's *at / on* five o'clock.
5 It's *from / on* five o'clock *at / until* eight o'clock.

2 Complete the table with the words in the box.

seven o'clock	16th July	18.15
Friday, 10th May	the swimming pool	
17.30–20.00	Wednesday	
two o'clock – four o'clock	4–5 pm	

on	at	from … until …

3 Write about you. Use *on, at, from* and *until*.

I get up at 7.00.
I've got history, maths and English on Fridays.
I'm at school from 9.00 until 3.00.

4 Complete the invitations with the words in the box.

at	from	on	until

Would you like to come to my party?

It's ⁰ ....on....... Thursday, 12th May
¹ .... the park,
² 16.00
³ .... 19.30.

Call Victor on
01298 479823.

COME TO MY
disco party!

It's ⁴ .... Jana's house
⁵ .... 6 pm ⁶ .... 9 pm
⁷ .... Saturday!

Email: jana@fgcool.com

1 Read the invitation. Answer the questions.

PARTY TIME!

TO	Jake
WHERE	My house
WHEN	Saturday, 3rd December
TIME	From 4.00 pm until 6.00 pm

FROM	Andrea
PHONE	0741 887 331
EMAIL	andrea@mymail.com

1 Who is the invitation from?
....

2 Who is the invitation for?
....

3 Which day is the party?
....

4 What time is the party?
....

2 Write an invitation to your party. Use Exercise 1 to help you.

....
....
....
....
....
....

7 MY DAY

VOCABULARY AND LISTENING

Daily activities

1 Look at the pictures. Complete the phrases with the words from the box.

catch	dinner	face	get	go to
have	school	shower	up	

1 get ....
2 have a ....
3 wash your ....
4 .... dressed
5 walk to ....
6 .... the bus to school
7 .... lunch
8 eat ....
9 .... bed

2 Which sentence is right (✓)?

1 A I clean my teeth and I get up. ☐
  B I get up and I clean my teeth. ☐

2 A I leave the house and I wash my face. ☐
  B I wash my face and leave the house. ☐

3 A I have breakfast and catch the bus to school. ☐
  B I catch the bus to school and have lunch. ☐

4 A I walk to school and I leave the house. ☐
  B I leave the house and I walk to school. ☐

5 A I get dressed and I catch the bus to school. ☐
  B I catch the bus to school and I get dressed. ☐

🔊 09 **3** Listen to the conversation between Connor and Abbie. Where is Rosa from?

🔊 09 **4** Listen again. Write *Yes* or *No*.

0 Rosa is 11 years old. .... *Yes* ....
1 Abbie gets up at six thirty. ....
2 Connor cleans his room on Saturdays. ....
3 Abbie likes eggs. ....
4 Abbie walks to school. ....
5 Connor catches the bus to school. ....

🔊 09 **5** Listen again. Choose the right pictures for Rosa.

1 A  B

2 A  B
  Saturdays ☐ every day ☐

3 A  B

4 A  B

1 Complete the text with the verbs in the box.

| catches | cleans | gets dressed |
| gets up | goes | has | leaves |

Holly ¹ _____ to school in Birmingham.
She ² _____ at 7.20 and she
³ _____ breakfast with her mum and
dad. Then she ⁴ _____ her teeth and
⁵ _____ . She ⁶ _____ the house
at 8.20 and she ⁷ _____ the bus to school.
Holly likes school!

2 Choose the correct word to complete the text.

Hi, I'm Pep and my dad is called Pablo. This
is our morning routine. Dad ¹ *get up / gets up*
at 6.15. He ² *wash / washes* his face and ³ *get
dressed / gets dressed*. I ⁴ *get up / gets up* at
6.30. I ⁵ *have / has* breakfast with Dad at 7.00.
After breakfast, Dad ⁶ *clean / cleans* his teeth.
Then I ⁷ *clean / cleans* my teeth! I ⁸ *leave /
leaves* the house at 8.30 and I ⁹ *walk / walks*
to school. Dad ¹⁰ *leave / leaves* the house at
9.00. He ¹¹ *catch / catches* the bus to work.
We ¹² *like / likes* our morning routine!

3 Complete the sentences with the correct form of
the verbs in the box.

| catch | get | have |
| leave | walk | wash |

1 I _____ up at 7.00.
2 I _____ my face and get dressed.
3 I _____ breakfast with my mum and
my brother at 7.30.
4 My mum and my brother _____ the
house at 8.00.
5 My brother _____ to school with his
friends.
6 My friends and I _____ the bus to
school.

4 Some sentences have mistakes in them. Write
right or *wrong*. Correct the wrong sentences.

0 He get up at 6.00.
  Wrong. He gets up at 6.00.
1 She get up at 6.30.
_____
2 He has a shower at 7.00.
_____
3 They have breakfast at 7.30.
_____
4 He catch the bus to school.
_____
5 She walk to school.
_____
6 They have lunch at 12.00.
_____
7 They does their homework after dinner.
_____
8 He go to bed at 10.00.
_____

Telling the time (2)

1 Match the times to the clocks.

0 It's half past four.   *B*

1 It's six o'clock.   ....

2 It's quarter past three.   ....

3 It's quarter to nine.   ....

4 It's half past seven.   ....

5 It's eight o'clock.   ....

6 It's five to two.   ....

7 It's ten to ten.   ....

8 It's quarter to six.   ....

2 Look at the pictures. Make sentences.

 11.45 pm

 8.00 am

 7.00 pm

 3.30 pm

 7.45 am

 6.50 pm

1 My cat sleeps	at eight o'clock	in the morning.
2 I catch the bus	at quarter to eight	in the evening.
3 My little brother goes to bed	at seven o'clock	at night.
4 Juan plays tennis	at half past three	in the afternoon.
5 We have breakfast	at ten to seven	in the evening.
6 My mum goes to English lessons	at quarter to twelve	in the morning.

3 Read the text. Who gets up first?

My family's day

Dad

Dad doesn't like the mornings. He says, 'Can't I stay in bed?' Dad works from home. He's tired in the mornings. He gets up at 7 am and has breakfast with us. In the evening, Dad makes dinner. I help him! We eat dinner at 6 pm. Dad works in the evening and goes to bed at 10 pm.

Mum

Mum gets up at half past five every morning! After that, she has a shower and gets dressed. She makes breakfast at 7 am. Mum leaves the house at 7.30 walks to school. Mum's a teacher, but she doesn't work at our school. In the evening, she reads books.

Hannah

Hannah is my sister. She's 13. She gets up at 6.30 in the morning and has a shower. Hannah catches the bus to school at 7.30. In the evening, she helps mum clean the kitchen and she talks to her friends on the internet.

Me

I'm Oscar. I'm 11. I get up fifteen minutes before breakfast. I leave the house at 7.45 in the morning. Hannah and I don't go to the same school. She catches the bus, but I walk. I like my walk to school. In the evening, I help Dad make dinner and I play board games.

4 Read the text again. Answer the questions.

0 Who makes dinner for the family?
Oscar's dad

1 What does Oscar's dad do at 10 pm?

....

2 Who gets up at 5.30?

....

3 What does Oscar's mum do in the evening?

....

4 What time does Hannah get up?

....

5 What does Hannah do at 7.30?

....

6 What does Oscar do at 7.45?

....

7 What does Oscar do in the evening?

....

Present simple ⊖

1 Complete the sentences. Use *don't* or *doesn't*.

0 I have breakfast with my mum and my sister.
   I *don't have breakfast* .... with my dad.
1 Amanda does her homework in the evening.
   She .... her homework
   in the morning.
2 My teacher works in a school.
   My teacher .... in a park.
3 I play football in the park with my friends.
   I .... football in my
   garden.
4 I clean my teeth in the morning and at night.
   I .... my teeth in the
   afternoon.
5 My brother sleeps in his bed.
   He .... on the floor.

2 Look at what Daniel does every week. Complete the sentences.

Daniel

Monday	clean my bedroom
Tuesday	make breakfast
Wednesday	make my bed
Thursday	walk to school
Friday	wash the car
Saturday	go to bed at 10.30 pm

0 He *doesn't clean* his bedroom on Friday.
1 He .... his bed on Tuesday.
2 He .... breakfast on Wednesday.
3 He .... the bus to school on
   Thursday.
4 He .... the car on Monday.
5 He .... to bed at ten o'clock
   on Saturday.

1 Read about Akiki's day. Write *Yes* or *No*. Correct the wrong sentences.

AKIKI'S DAY

This is Akiki. He's 12 years old and he lives in Uganda in Africa with his sister and his parents. Their house has got two rooms. He gets up at 6 am and has breakfast at 6.30 am. At 7 am Akiki goes to school. He walks to school with his friend Kizza but some of their friends don't go to school. In the evening, Akiki does his homework and at night he is very tired.

0 Akiki lives in a big house.
   No. He lives in a small house.
1 He lives with his family.
   ....
2 Akiki gets up at six o'clock.
   ....
3 He has breakfast at quarter past six.
   ....
4 He goes to school at seven o'clock.
   ....
5 Akiki catches the bus to school.
   ....
6 Akiki does his homework in the morning.
   ....

2 Read about Caitlin's day, then write a description of her day. Use the text in Exercise 1 to help you.

Morning	
7.00	get up
7.30	have breakfast
8.00–12.00	play the guitar with guitar teacher
Afternoon	
12.00–1.00	have lunch
1.00–5.00	have music lessons
5.00–6.00	have dinner
Evening	
6.00–7.00	do homework
7.00–9.00	talk with friends, read, watch TV
10.00	go to bed

Caitlin's day

....

....

....

....

....

8 AT SCHOOL

VOCABULARY AND LISTENING

School subjects

1 Look at the pictures and write the words.

| 1 .... | 2 .... | 3 .... | 4 .... | 5 .... |

| 6 .... | 7 .... | 8 .... | 9 .... | 10 .... |

2 Read the sentences. Write the school subjects from Exercise 1.

1 Ready? Go! Run and kick the ball.
....

2 Look at your computer.
....

3 Have you got your guitar, Marco?
....

4 Moscow is in Russia.
....

5 734 + 124 = 858
....

6 I am, you are, he is, she is …
....

7 OK, everyone, please paint a picture of a horse.
....

8 In the year 1812, Napoleon Bonaparte of France …
....

9 Water is also called H_2O.
....

10 *Bonjour!*
....

 3 Listen to the conversation. Which are Ellen's favourite subjects?

 4 Listen again. Complete Ellen's timetable.

	Monday	Tuesday	Wednesday	Thursday	Friday
am	0 _maths_	1	2	3	4 ....
	maths	science	history	science	history
	Lunch				
pm	English	geography	science	geography	English
	5	PE	IT	PE	6 ....

 5 Listen again. Are the sentences right (✓) or wrong (✗)?

0 Ellen isn't happy with her timetable. ✓
1 Maths is Ryan's favourite subject. ....
2 Ellen says maths is important. ....
3 Ellen's lessons start at 8.00. ....
4 Ellen's lessons finish at 2.00. ....
5 Ryan has got English on Monday mornings. ....

1 Complete the questions with *Do* or *Does*.

0 _____*Does*_____ our friend have lunch at school?

1 _____ your parents speak English?

2 _____ your school have a film club?

3 _____ your teacher catch the bus to school?

4 _____ you have PE on Fridays?

5 _____ your friends do their homework?

6 _____ your sister go to school on Saturdays?

7 _____ your brother go to your school?

8 _____ you have art on Wednesdays?

2 Match the questions from Exercise 1 with the answers below.

a No, he doesn't. He goes home for it.

b Yes, they do. They do it before they have dinner.

c Yes, I do. It's my favourite subject! I like painting and drawing.

d No, she doesn't! She plays football with her friends.

e No, she doesn't. She walks to school.

f Yes, it does. We go every Friday evening.

g Yes, he does. We walk to school together.

h Yes, they do. They can speak Chinese, too.

i No, we don't. We have it on Mondays. I don't like PE.

0

3 Write the questions.

0 Eve / geography / Mondays?
Does Eve have geography on Mondays?

1 Eve / art / Mondays?

2 Eve / IT / Mondays?

3 Jack / history / Tuesdays?

4 Jack / maths / Tuesdays?

5 Jack / PE / afternoon?

6 Eve and Jack / science / morning?

7 Eve and Jack / music / Mondays?

8 Eve and Jack / English / morning?

4 Look at the school timetables. Answer the questions in Exercise 3.

0 *No, she doesn't. She has it on Tuesdays.*

1 _____

2 _____

3 _____

4 _____

5 _____

6 _____

7 _____

8 _____

Eve

	Monday	Tuesday
9.05	science	geography
10.05	PE	history
BREAK		
11.20	maths	French
LUNCH		
13.30	IT	English
14.20	music	art

Jack

	Monday	Tuesday
9.05	science	geography
10.05	PE	history
BREAK		
11.20	maths	French
LUNCH		
13.30	IT	English
14.20	music	art

VOCABULARY AND READING

Words with two meanings

1 Match the verbs with the pairs of definitions.

1 come to/from
2 get
3 meet
4 see
5 think
6 catch

a believe something to be true
b have an opinion about something
c go to a place or to where a person is
d be from a place, e.g. a city or a country
e take hold of something that is moving through the air, e.g. a ball
f get on bus or train to go somewhere
g arrive somewhere
h receive something
i use your eyes
j visit or meet someone
k see and speak to someone for the first time
l see someone at a place and time

2 Complete the sentences. Use the verbs from Exercise 1. Use some verbs twice.

0 Hello, children! _____*Meet*_____ your new teacher. Her name's Linda.

1 I always _____ my friends in the park on Saturday afternoons.

2 I'm French. I _____ from Paris.

3 Would you like to _____ to my party on Saturday?

4 What do you _____ of my new coat? Do you like it?

5 I _____ the film starts at 6 o'clock. Let's go!

6 Can you _____ that boy over there, Mum? He goes to my school.

7 I _____ to school at 8.45 am.

8 Do you _____ the bus to school?

3 Read the dialogue. Which subject do Ava and Luiz both have on a Tuesday?

Ava: Hi, Luiz.
Luiz: Hi, Ava. Good to talk to you again. How are you?
Ava: I'm fine, thanks! And you?
Luiz: I'm OK. But I'm tired after school.
Ava: Me too!
Luiz: What time do you go to school in the morning?
Ava: Most days I catch the bus at 8.30 with my sister. School starts at 9.00. How about you? When time do you go?
Luiz: Oh, it's very early in Brazil! Lessons start at 7 am!
Ava: 7 am!
Luiz: Yes, Monday to Friday. But I like the mornings.
Ava: Do you catch the bus to school?
Luiz: No, I don't. I walk to school with my brothers. What about lunch, Ava? Do you have lunch at school?
Ava: Yes, I do. What about you?
Luiz: I never have lunch at school! I have lunch at home with my family. What do you do in the afternoons?
Ava: I stay at school. I've got more lessons!
Luiz: Really? We don't have lessons in the afternoon!
Ava: Wow! I like that. We always have lessons in the afternoon in Canada. The school day finishes at 3.30. After that, I often meet my friends in a café. What subjects do you like, Luiz?
Luiz: Um … I think my favourite subjects are English and PE. What are yours?
Ava: History is my favourite. I'm good at it. We have it on Mondays and Wednesday afternoons. I think history is a very interesting subject. I like science too. We have that on Tuesdays and Thursdays.
Luiz: We have science on Tuesdays and Fridays. I don't like science very much. But I like school. I've got lots of friends and my teachers are good.

4 Read the texts again. Write *Ava* or *Luiz*.

0 _____*Luiz*_____ goes to school at seven o'clock.
1 _____ catches the bus to school.
2 _____ doesn't have lunch at home.
3 _____ goes to school in the afternoon.
4 _____ often meets friends after school.
5 _____ thinks history is interesting.
6 _____ doesn't like science.

1 Complete the questions with the words in the box.

> how often   what   when
> where   ~~who~~   why

0 _____*Who*_____ is your favourite teacher?

1 _____ is your favourite sport?

2 _____ do you live?

3 _____ does school start in the morning?

4 _____ do you talk to your friends?

5 _____ do you like English?

2 Match the questions in Exercise 1 to the answers.

a In Rome. ....

b Every day! ....

c Because I like learning languages. ....

d At 9 am. ....

e Tennis. ....

f Mr Black. ....

3 Put the words in the right order to make questions.

1 TV / often / How / do / you / watch / ?

....

2 do / Where / play / football / you / ?

....

3 When / up / you / do / get / ?

....

4 do / you / What / the / at / do / weekend ?

....

5 English / Who / your / is / teacher / ?

....

6 you / like / swimming / do / Why / ?

....

4 Answer the questions in Exercise 2 for you.

1 ....

2 ....

3 ....

4 ....

5 ....

6 ....

1 Complete the questions in the questionnaire.

The school questionnaire

0 _____*What*_____ 's your name?
Thomas Martin

1 _____ are you from?
Paris, France

2 _____ do you go to school?
at 8 am

3 _____ 's your favourite subject?
art

4 _____ is it your favourite subject?
because I like painting

5 _____ often do you have art at school?
three days a week

6 _____ do you do your homework – in the evening or in the morning?
in the evening

2 Maria goes to Thomas's school. Read about Maria then write about Thomas. Use the school questionnaire and text about Maria to help you.

Maria and school

Maria Dupont comes from Paris in France. She is 13 years old. She goes to school at 8 am. Her favourite subject is science. She likes science because she is interested in the world. She has science at school two days a week. Maria does her homework in the evening.

Thomas and school

....

....

....

....

....

....

9 FEELING GOOD

VOCABULARY AND LISTENING

Sports and activities

1 Complete the words for sports and activities.

1 hoc_____ _____
2 d_____ing
3 ru_____ _____ _____ _____
4 f_____ll
5 s_____ing
6 t_____i s

2 Write the name of the sport under the picture.

1 _____

2 _____

3 _____

4 _____

3 Complete the conversations with activities from Exercise 1.

A: Do you like ⁰ _____*football*_____?
B: No, I don't. What about you?
A: Yes, I do! I like FC Barcelona.

A: Do you like ¹ _____?
B: Yes, I do. It's my favourite sport! I like Rafa Nadal and Garbiñe Muguruza.

A: Do you go ² _____?
B: Yes, I do. I go five times a week. There's a great pool near my house.

A: Do you go ³ _____?
B: No, I don't. How about you?
A: Yes, I do. There's a big park behind my school. I run there with my sister.

A: What's your favourite sport?
B: ⁴ _____. I play it with my friends at the weekend.

◁)) 11 4 Listen to four students talking. What are they talking about?

◁)) 11 5 Listen again. Tick the things the students are good at.

1 **Charlie** **A** dancing ☐ **B** football ☐
2 **Anna** **A** hockey ☐ **B** running ☐
3 **Ed** **A** swimming ☐ **B** baseball ☐
4 **Dana** **A** hockey ☐ **B** basketball ☐

◁)) 11 6 Listen again. Which sentence is right (✓)?

1 **A** Charlie likes table tennis. ☐
  B Charlie likes hockey. ☐

2 **A** Anna likes badminton. ☐
  B Anna likes swimming. ☐

3 **A** Ed sometimes goes running. ☐
  B Ed goes running every week. ☐

4 **A** Dana likes table tennis. ☐
  B Dana likes football. ☐

5 **A** Dana sometimes plays hockey. ☐
  B Dana never plays hockey. ☐

GRAMMAR   *like* ➕ ➖

1 Choose the correct words.

1 I like going to school, but I *like / don't like* doing homework.
2 My friends *like / don't like* running. They run every morning before school!
3 My sister *likes / doesn't like* swimming. She's very happy in the water.
4 My brother *likes / doesn't like* playing football, but he likes watching it on TV.
5 I *like / don't like* eating chocolate. I eat it every weekend!
6 I *like / don't like* playing badminton, but I like playing tennis.
7 I *like / don't like* your new camera. It's very nice.

2 Match to make sentences.

1 Marco doesn't like playing football and
2 Jake doesn't like singing but
3 Marisa likes running and
4 Ben and Amy don't like running and
5 Sam and Hugo like swimming and
6 Ana likes singing but

a he doesn't like playing basketball.
b she likes playing basketball.
c they like playing football.
d they don't like swimming.
e she doesn't like dancing.
f he likes dancing.

3 Look at the table. Complete the sentences.

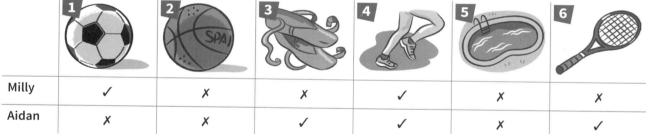

	1	2	3	4	5	6
Milly	✓	✗	✗	✓	✗	✗
Aidan	✗	✗	✓	✓	✗	✓

1 Milly _____ football.
  Aidan _____ football.
2 Milly _____ basketball.
  Aidan _____ basketball.
3 Milly _____ dancing.
  Aidan _____ dancing.
4 Milly _____ running.
  Aidan _____ running.
5 Milly _____ swimming.
  Aidan _____ swimming.
6 Milly _____ tennis.
  Aidan _____ tennis.

4 Write positive or negative sentences.

1 Robin / swimming   ✗
2 Tom / basketball   ✗
3 Sima / dancing   ✓
4 Mum and Dad / running   ✗
5 My friends / baseball   ✓
6 My sister / reading   ✓
7 My brother / drawing   ✓
8 Clara / send / text messages   ✗
9 Marco and Gianni / watch TV   ✗
10 Isabella / ride horses   ✓

5 Write about what you like and don't like. Use the words in the box.

basketball	dancing	football
running	table tennis	

_____
_____
_____

VOCABULARY AND READING

Health

1 Complete the phrases with the words in the box.

better	feel	feel	for	you

1 good _____ you
2 feel _____
3 is not good for _____
4 _____ fine
5 _____ well

2 Complete the conversations with the phrases from Exercise 1.

0 A: Why do you eat lots of apples?
B: Because they're
_____*good for you*_____!

1 A: I eat chocolate and biscuits every day. Is that OK?
B: Don't eat them every day. It
_____.

2 A: I'm tired. I can't do my homework.
B: Go for a walk. You'll
_____ after that.

3 A: I don't eat fruit and vegetables. Sometimes I don't feel well.
B: It's good for you to eat fruit and vegetables. Eat them and you'll
_____.

4 A: I don't have breakfast. And in the morning at school I don't feel well.
B: Oh, have breakfast! You'll
_____.

3 Answer the questions with sentences about you.

1 What makes you feel well?
Swimming makes me feel well. I always feel better.

2 What is good for you?
....

3 What isn't good for you?
....

4 Read the text. What time does the family eat breakfast?

What we have for breakfast

Laura is 12 years old and is from Cambridge. She tells us about breakfast in her family.

Some people don't have breakfast, but my mum and dad say a healthy breakfast is good for us – we feel well.

My family has breakfast at seven o'clock every morning. I eat some fruit and some bread. I drink some water too. I don't eat biscuits. I like them but my mum says they're not good for me.

Raquel and Paula are my sisters. Raquel likes milk and drinks lots of it. She has bread and butter for breakfast and lots of fruit. Paula doesn't like bread. She has fruit and some water.

My brother's name is Will. Will eats eggs and bread and butter for breakfast. He has orange juice too. Will likes fruit, but he doesn't like it at breakfast. He eats fruit at lunch.

Mum has fruit, yoghurt, and milk for breakfast. Dad has some bread and butter. He has some cheese too. He doesn't drink milk. He doesn't like it. He drinks water.

5 Read the text again. Match the descriptions to the people.

1 Raquel   a eggs, bread and orange juice
2 Paula   b fruit, yoghurt and milk
3 Will   c milk, bread and fruit
4 Mum   d bread, cheese and water
5 Dad   e fruit and water
6 Laura   f fruit, bread and water

1 Choose the correct words to complete the sentences.

1 I like eating biscuits but they aren't good for *me / him*.
2 I play tennis with my friends. It's good for *her / us*.
3 I play the guitar but I'm not very good at *him / it*.
4 My sister eats vegetables. They're good for *him / her*.
5 My brother sleeps for eight hours every night. It's good for *him / her*.
6 My parents like running. It's good for *them / her*.
7 Eat lots of fruit. It's good for *it / you*.

2 Change the <u>underlined</u> words. Write *him, her, it, us, them* or *you*.

0 I like football. I'm good at <u>football</u>.   *it*
1 My brother eats lots of sugar. It's not good for <u>my brother</u>.
2 My friends and I walk to school. It's good for <u>my friends and me</u>.
3 My sister drinks lots of water. It's good for <u>my sister</u>.
4 My parents eat some fruit for breakfast. It's good for <u>my parents</u>.
5 Play lots of sport. It's good for <u>you and your friends</u>.
6 My mum eats a lot of fruit. It's good for <u>my mum.</u>
7 My sister plays basketball. She's good at <u>basketball</u>.
8 My dad eats a lot of chocolate. It isn't good for <u>my dad</u>.
9 I like running. I'm good at <u>running</u>.
10 My friends go swimming five days a week. It's good for <u>my friends</u>.

1 Read the text. What is it about?

Hello! My name is Luca and I like doing lots of things in my free time. I like reading books and swimming. I read every day and I swim five days a week. I like watching music videos, but I don't like playing computer games. I don't like cooking, but I like eating. I like eating chocolate, but eating lots of chocolate isn't good for me!

2 Read the text again. Write *Yes, he does* or *No, he doesn't*.

1 Does Luca like reading books?

2 Does he like swimming?

3 Does he like watching music videos?

4 Does he like playing computer games?

5 Does he like cooking?

6 Does he like eating chocolate?

3 Answer the questions for you in the questionnaire. Write *Yes, I do* or *No, I don't*.

What do you like doing in your free time?

1 Do you like reading books?
2 Do you like playing computer games?
3 Do you like cooking?
4 Do you like eating chocolate?
5 Do you like swimming?
6 Do you like watching music videos?

4 Write about what you like doing in your free time. Use the text in Exercise 1 and your answers in Exercise 3 to help you.

VOCABULARY AND LISTENING

After-school activities

1 Put the letters in the right order to make school clubs.

0 lfmi
film

1 gyoa

2 odju

3 radam

4 nogicd

5 oeyrcko

6 iadggnnre

7 slttaiech

8 daobr msega

9 eohrs-iigrdn

2 Complete the sentences.

0 It's ___*coding*___ club after school today. Mr Macmillan says we can use the new laptops.

1 Hello everyone and welcome to _____ club. What would you like to watch this afternoon – *Star Wars: The Force Awakens* or *The Last Jedi*?

2 Can we play chess in _____ club?

3 Are you ready for _____ club? Today, we are learning some Italian phrases.

4 We run in _____ club. We have races, too!

5 Do you grow vegetables in _____ club?

3 Listen to Miss Doyle talk to her class. Which club does everyone like?

4 Listen again. Complete the timetable.

Timetable for after-school clubs				
Monday	**Tuesday**	**Wednesday**	**Thursday**	**Friday**
0 ___*judo*___	3 _____	5 _____	6 _____	7 _____
1 _____	4 _____			8 _____
2 _____				9 _____

5 Listen again. Write *Yes* or *No.* Correct the wrong sentences.

0 Judo club is at four o'clock. ___*Yes*___

1 Yoga starts before athletics club. _____

2 Athletics club starts at 4.15. _____

3 The school doesn't have a coding club. _____

4 Horse-riding club is at half-past four. _____

5 There is one club on Friday. _____

1 Look at the pictures. Put the verbs in brackets in the correct form.

1 Julia's _____ (ride) a horse.

2 Her brother is _____ (kick) a ball.

3 Her sister isn't _____ (write) a letter.
She's _____ (do) her homework.

4 Her mum is _____ (make) lunch and
her dad is _____ (sit) on a chair.

2 Complete the sentences with the words from the box. Use the correct form.

cook	do	kick	make	paint
play	talk	watch	write	

0 I'm in my room. I *'m making* my bed.
1 My sister's in the living room. She
_____ a text message.
2 My brother's in his bedroom. He
_____ a board game with his friend.
3 Dad's in the kitchen. He _____ to his
friend on his phone.
4 Mum and her friend are in the living room.
They _____ a picture.
5 My friends Max and Bill are at home.
They _____ their homework.
6 My aunt and uncle _____ pasta.
7 My friend Jack _____ TV.
8 My friend Julia is _____ a ball in
the garden.

3 Write the negative form of the sentences from Exercise 2.

0 *I'm not in my room. I'm not making my bed.*
1 _____
2 _____
3 _____
4 _____
5 _____
6 _____
7 _____
8 _____

4 Look at the pictures. Write sentences.

1 Daniella is my sister. She likes music.
_____ (she / dance)
in the street.
_____ (she / play) the guitar.
2 Miguel is my brother.
_____ (he / play) basketball.
_____ (he / run) in the park.
3 Tomas and Juan are my friends.
_____ (they / sing).
_____ (they / swim).
4 You're a student.
_____ (you / do) your
homework.
_____ (you / make) your bed.

Jobs around the house

1 Complete the sentences with the words from the box. Use the correct form.

clean	cooking	dog	washing-up
feed	shopping	tidy	

0 **A:** Mum, the cat's hungry.
   B: Can you _____feed_____ it, please?

1 **B:** One moment, Dad. I'm doing the
   _____.

2 **A:** Where's Chloe?
   B: She's in the kitchen. She's cooking
   the _____.

3 **B:** Can you help me carry the _____?
   These bags are very heavy.

4 **A:** Where's Mum?
   B: She's walking the _____.

5 **A:** Oh, look at the bath!
   B: Yes, it's time to _____ it.

6 **A:** Look at these clothes on the floor!
   _____ your room, please.

2 Choose the correct words.

1 *do / make* your bed
2 *do / make* the housework
3 *do / make* a cake
4 *do / make* the washing
5 *do / make* breakfast
6 *do / make* lunch

3 Look at the pictures and write sentences with *do* or *make*.

0 *He's making his bed.*
1 _____
2 _____
3 _____
4 _____
5 _____

4 Read the email. Which three people have their birthday today?

Hi Chen,

How are you? What are you doing now?

It's hot here today. I'm in the park with my friends. We're having a big party. I'm 13 today, Chen! But it's not only my birthday – it's Ingrid's and David's too!

I'm writing you this email on my new smartphone. It's a birthday present from my parents. I'm sitting on a bench near the big trees and I can see all my friends.

Alex and Andres are dancing to some loud music. They're very good at it. Carlos isn't dancing. He can't dance very well. He's playing football with Camilo and Julian.

Ingrid and Diego don't like football. They are playing tennis. Ingrid is good at it, but Diego isn't!

Who else can I see? Oh, yes – Luisa! She's sitting under a tree. She's talking to David. David is next to her. He's sitting on the grass. They're good friends.

Write soon.

Love from Gabriela x

5 Read the email again. Answer the questions.

1 Where is Gabriela?
_____

2 How old is Gabriela today?
_____

3 What is Gabriela's birthday present?
_____

4 Who is good at dancing?
_____

5 Who can't dance well?
_____

6 Is Diego good at tennis?
_____

7 Where is Luisa?
_____

8 Where is David?
_____

9 Who is David talking to?
_____

GRAMMAR Present continuous ❓

1 Complete the questions.

1 A: Hello. I'm Abby. I'm in my bedroom.
   B: _____ doing your homework?
   A: Yes, I am.

2 A: My brother is in the kitchen.
   B: _____ making lunch?
   A: No, he isn't. He's making a cake.

3 A: My mum isn't in the house.
   B: _____ washing the car?
   A: Yes, she is. It's very dirty!

4 A: Meg and Poppy like music.
   B: _____ singing?
   A: No, they aren't. They're dancing.

5 A: William is my brother. He's in his bedroom.
   B: _____ making his bed?
   A: No, he isn't! He's playing a board game.

6 A: Laura and Beth are my friends. They like sport.
   B: _____ running?
   A: Yes they are.

7 A: I'm a student.
   B: _____ doing your maths homework?
   A: No, I'm not. I'm doing my English homework.

2 Put the words in the right order to make questions. Then write short answers.

0 are / friends / your / playing / football
   Are your friends playing football? ?
   No, they aren't. ✗

1 bed / Are / you / your / making
   _____ ?
   _____ ✗

2 your / brother / the / kitchen / cleaning / Is
   _____ ?
   _____ ✓

3 your / friends / making / Are / lunch
   _____ ?
   _____ ✓

4 drawing / a / picture / Are / you
   _____ ?
   _____ ✗

5 Is / sister / breakfast / your / eating
   _____ ?
   _____ ✓

WRITING

1 Read the text. Find three spelling mistakes and two grammar mistakes.

1 _____   4 _____
2 _____   5 _____
3 _____

My Life – Claudia's Blog

Wednesday, 14 March. Time: 13.01

This blog post is about my family. I've got a big family – Mum, Dad, one brother and two sisters. What are they doin at this moment? Well, Dad is cleanng the kitchen and Mum is writting an email. My sister Giorgia is playing the guitar – she's very good! My sister Sofia are eating a sandwich – she's always hungry! My brother Lorenzo is in his bedroom. He's doing his homework. What am I doing? I'm writing this blog post! What is you and your family doing?

2 Read the text again. Write *Yes, she is* or *No, she isn't*. Correct the wrong sentences.

1 Her dad is cleaning the kitchen.
_____

2 Her mum is writing a letter.
_____

3 Sofia is eating a sandwich.
_____

4 Lorenzo is in the living room.
_____

5 Lorenzo is doing his homework.
_____

6 Claudia is writing an email.
_____

3 Write about what you and your family are doing. Use Claudia's blog post to help you.

VOCABULARY AND LISTENING

Entertainment

1 Look at the pictures. Write the numbers.

_4_ Hi. My name's Brad. I'm a famous person!
___ I'm a singer in a band.
___ I write the songs.
___ We've got lots of fans.
___ Look. Here's our picture in the newspaper.
___ We give lots of concerts.
___ We sometimes sing on a TV show.
___ They are making a movie about us.

2 Complete the sentences with the words in the box.

band	concert	famous	fans
movie	newspapers	song	

1 Do your parents read _____ or read the news online?
2 Look at all these people! This singer's got lots of _____ .
3 Look. Your mum is on TV. She's a _____ person!
4 Do you want to watch a _____ ? We can go to the new cinema!
5 Abbie sings, Erin plays the guitar and Luke plays the piano. They can start a _____ .
6 Do you know the _____ ? You can listen to it on YouTube.
7 Lana's band is playing in a big _____ on Saturday. Do you want to go?

🔊 13 **3** Listen to the conversation. What do the speakers decide to do?

🔊 13 **4** Listen again. Which sentence is right (✓)?

1 a Izzy sings. ☐
  b Izzy plays the piano. ☐
2 a Anya plays the violin. ☐
  b Anya doesn't play the piano. ☐
3 a Robin plays the guitar. ☐
  b Robin doesn't play the guitar. ☐
4 a Izzy writes songs. ☐
  b Anya writes songs. ☐
5 a Robin doesn't want to start a band. ☐
  b Robin wants to start a band. ☐

🔊 13 **5** Listen again. Who says these words? Write _I_ for Izzy, _A_ for Anya and _R_ for Robin.

1 Do you play an instrument, Izzy? ____
2 Yes. I can play the piano and the violin. ____
3 I play the guitar, but I can't play it very well. ____
4 Anya writes her own songs. ____
5 I write songs all the time, Robin. ____
6 What's the name of our band? ____
7 My favourite colour is blue and Anya loves cats. ____

1 Put the words in the right order to make sentences.

1 sometimes / friend / horses / rides / My

2 always / homework / I / my / do

3 sister / swimming / goes / often / My

4 brother / My / sings / always / in / the / shower

5 sometimes / play / I / games / board

6 watch / I / always / favourite / my / show / TV

7 dad / often / newspaper / My / reads / a

8 goes / My / never / to / friend / concerts

9 TV / never / My / mum / watches

2 Rewrite the sentences with the word in brackets in the correct place.

0 I get the bus to school.   (always)
   I (always) get the bus to school.

1 I play football.   (never)

2 Laura plays in her friend's band.   (sometimes)

3 We work on laptops in school.   (often)

4 You do your homework.   (sometimes)

5 I listen to music in my room.   (always)

6 My sister goes swimming.   (sometimes)

7 My friends go to the cinema.   (never)

8 We have pizza at the weekend.   (often)

3 Choose the correct adverbs.

1 I *never / often* do my homework in the morning. I always do it after school.

2 We *always / often* go to my grandparents' house on Sundays. We go there for lunch every week.

3 I *sometimes / always* make breakfast for my little sister and sometimes my dad makes it.

4 I *always / often* go to the cinema on Saturday evenings, but sometimes I stay at home and watch films with my family.

5 I *always / sometimes* walk to school with my friends. We never catch the bus or go by car!

6 My brother loves swimming, but I *often / never* go to the pool. I don't like swimming.

7 We *often / always* have pasta for dinner. We have it two or three times a week.

4 Complete the sentences about you with *always, often, sometimes* or *never*.

1 I _____ play in a band.
2 I _____ watch TV.
3 I _____ read a newspaper.
4 I _____ meet famous people.
5 I _____ sing songs.
6 I _____ watch movies.
7 I _____ go to concerts.
8 I _____ read books.
9 I _____ ride a horse.
10 I _____ do my homework.
11 I _____ eat chocolate.
12 I _____ go swimming.

VOCABULARY AND READING

Technology

1 Look at the pictures. Write the words.

1 d_____ c_____
2 t_____
3 s_____
4 l_____
5 f_____ t_____
6 s_____ s_____

2 Complete the sentences with the words in the box.

> count your steps   look at websites
> play games   read and send emails
> read and send texts   stream music
> take photos   watch films

1 I _____ in the park with my digital camera.
2 I've got a new smartphone.
   I _____ every day.
3 Fitness trackers are great. You walk around and they _____.
4 I listen to Ariana Grande and Billie Eilish.
   I _____ on the internet.
5 Have you got Netflix? It's a great place to _____.
6 My dad has got a very old laptop. He uses it to _____ for work.
7 Do you use your smartphone to _____. I don't, but my brother does. He always asks me to play them with him.
8 I like to _____ on my tablet. My favourite one is about cars.

3 Read the website posts. Has everyone got a smartphone?

What we *think* of TECH

I love it! I've got a smartphone, a tablet, a laptop and a fitness tracker. Every day I look at websites, send lots of texts and stream music. I can't live without technology. I go online after school and I talk to my friends all night. Everyone's got their own YouTube channel – it's brilliant!

Yang

I've got my smartphone with me all the time – at home, on the bus, on the street. I talk to my friends online all the time. We stream music, play games and watch videos. My brother got a digital camera, but I use my smartphone to take photos.

Inés

Technology's OK. I've got a smartphone and a laptop. I sometimes use them to look at websites to help me with homework. My sister's got a fitness tracker, but I haven't got one. I don't want to know how many steps I do when I walk!

Olga

My friends don't understand, but I don't like smartphones. Why don't people put them down and talk to each other? I've got a computer at home and I use to look at websites, but I haven't got a smartphone. There's one thing I like – my fitness tracker. I use it when I walk and run.

Ryan

4 Read the text again. Write *Yes* or *No*. Correct the wrong sentences.

1 Yang has got a laptop.
_____

2 Yang and his friends like YouTube.
_____

3 Inés never has her smartphone with her.
_____

4 Inés takes photos with her phone.
_____

5 Olga's brother has got a fitness tracker.
_____

6 Ryan loves smartphones.
_____

7 Ryan has a computer at home.
_____

1 Complete the questions with *much* or *many*.

1 How _____ photos have you got in your bedroom?
2 How _____ homework do you do in a week?
3 How _____ emails do you send in a month?
4 How _____ text messages do you write in a day?
5 How _____ fruit do you eat in a week?
6 How _____ eggs do you eat in a week?
7 How _____ computer games have you got?
8 How _____ water do you drink in a day?
9 How _____ chocolate do you eat at the weekend?

2 Match the questions in Exercise 1 with the answers below.

a Not much. I prefer milk or juice.
b I haven't got any pictures, but my sister's got lots of her friends.
c I don't send any. My friends and I talk on social media.
d Not much. My teacher usually gives it to us once or twice a week.
e Lots! I love them. I have them with bread.
f A lot. I usually eat bananas and oranges.
g My sister's got lots of games, but I haven't got any.
h Oh, I don't know. Lots! I use my phone all the time.
i I don't eat any, but my dad loves chocolate.

3 Complete the conversations. Write *any, lots, many* or *much*.

1 A: How _____ fruit do you eat?
  B: I eat _____. I like it. My friend doesn't eat _____. She doesn't like it!

2 A: How _____ books does your mum read in a month?
  B: I don't know, but she reads _____ of emails!

3 A: How _____ homework do you do on the computer?
  B: I do _____ but my little brother doesn't do _____.

4 A: How _____ TV shows do you watch in a week?
  B: I never watch TV. But my brother watches _____.

5 A: How _____ chocolate do you eat?
  B: I don't eat any chocolate. But my mum eats _____.

6 A: How _____ board games have you got?
  B: _____! I love playing them!

7 A: How _____ emails do you send every day?
  B: I don't send _____ but my dad sends lots. I send lots of texts.

1 Read the text about Wang. What's her favourite thing to eat?

Wang love music. She listens to it every night for about two hours. She don't watch any videos online, but her friends watch a lot. She doesn't send any text messages because she haven't got a phone. She play football twice a week and she eats lots of chocolate. It's her favourite thing to eat!

2 Read the text again. Circle and correct four grammar mistakes.

1 _____
2 _____
3 _____
4 _____

3 Match the questions to Wang's answers.

1 How much music do you listen to in a week?
2 How many online videos do you watch in a week?
3 How many text messages do you send in a week?
4 How much sport do you do in a week?
5 How much chocolate do you eat in a week?

a I don't send any. I haven't got a phone.
b Oh, lots. It's my favourite thing to eat.
c I play football twice a week.
d I don't watch any, but my friends watch lots.
e Lots. I listen to it for about two hours every night.

4 Answer the questions in Exercise 3 about your friend.

1 _____
2 _____
3 _____
4 _____
5 _____

5 Write about a friend. Use the text in Exercise 1 and your answers in Exercise 3 to help you.

_____
_____
_____
_____

12 WORKING LIFE

VOCABULARY AND LISTENING

Jobs

1 Match the people with what they do.

1	journalist	**a**	plays music
2	nurse	**b**	grows food
3	footballer	**c**	helps people feel better
4	waiter	**d**	works in a café or restaurant
5	musician	**e**	travels a lot on the roads
6	farmer	**f**	writes news stories
7	photographer	**g**	wears special clothes and stops fires
8	doctor	**h**	helps doctors look after people
9	firefighter	**i**	runs a lot
10	lorry driver	**j**	takes pictures

2 Complete the sentences with the words from Exercise 1.

1 My brother wants to be a _____. He wants to grow vegetables.

2 My uncle drives all over the UK. He's a _____.

3 Jon's sister's a _____. Look at this. Isn't it great? It's one of her photos!

4 My friend's a _____. She's in a band. Would you like to hear one of her songs?

5 Mum's a _____. She works in a hospital.

6 A _____ wears a big coat, a helmet, boots and gloves.

7 I want to be a _____ when I leave school. I want to write news reports for a website.

8 My sister's a _____. She wants to play for Real Madrid.

9 My friend wants to work in a hospital. He doesn't want to be a doctor, he wants to be a _____.

10 Toni's a _____. He works in his mother's restaurant.

3 Listen to the conversation. What jobs do Charlie and Amelia want to do?

4 Listen again. Complete the sentences with Charlie or Amelia.

0 _Charlie_ 's mum is a journalist.

1 _____ would like to write for a website.

2 _____ wants to be a footballer.

3 _____ plays for the school football team.

4 _____ 's mum is a doctor.

5 _____ 's dad is a lorry driver.

6 _____ 's dad is a photographer.

5 Listen again. Put the sentences in the order you hear them.

A What would you like to do, Amelia? _____

B I think that's an interesting job. _____

C Mum's a doctor. _____

D Do you want to write for that newspaper? _____

E What do you want to do when you leave school, Charlie? _1_

F Do you play football for the school team? _____

G His photos are on every wall of the house! _____

H Does anyone in your family play football? _____

1   Choose the correct words.

1. *Do you walk / Are you walking* to school every day?
2. Hi, Jamie! What *do you do / are you doing* at the moment?
3. I *play / I'm playing* football every Sunday morning.
4. Mum *doesn't work / isn't working* now. She's watching TV with Dad.
5. My uncle always *goes / is going* to France in the summer.
6. We *have / are having* a picnic in the garden today.
7. My brother and sister *make / are making* pizza for dinner now. I'm hungry!
8. What time *do you go / are you going* to school on Mondays?
9. Dad *works / is working* in London today.

2   Correct the sentences.

1. I can't come to the park, Jon, I'm do my homework.

2. Dad isn't at work now, he cleans the kitchen.

3. Layla! What's that noise? What do you do?

4. What time are you getting up every day?

5. Every morning I'm eating bread for breakfast.

6. My sister doesn't play the guitar now. She's watching TV.

7. Are you sending text messages every day?

8. Every Saturday I'm playing tennis with my friends.

9. I eat a big ice cream now. It's very nice!

10. I'm using my smartphone every day.

3   Complete the sentences. Use two verbs in each box.

0

~~are walking~~	~~doesn't walk~~
don't walk	is walking

My sister *doesn't walk* to school on Mondays.
Sue and Lynn *are walking* in the park today.

1

are dancing	is dancing
dance	dances

My dad never _____ in the street.
Julie's happy! She _____ in the house!

2

are eating	is eating	eat	eats

My friends always _____ lots of fruit.
Today's my birthday. We _____ pizza in a restaurant.

3

aren't writing	isn't writing
don't write	doesn't write

Cathy's teacher _____ on the board now.
My mum and dad _____ emails every day.

4

am making	is making
don't make	doesn't make

I _____ a sandwich now.
My brother _____ his bed every morning.

5

are doing	is doing	do	does

Josh and his family _____ the cleaning every week.
You _____ your homework now.

6

am playing	are playing
play	plays

I sometimes _____ board games in the afternoon.
My friends _____ basketball today.

In a café

1 Look at the photos. Write the words.

0 b *ottle* **1** s____ **2** s____ **3** c____ **4** s____

5 p____ **6** b____ **7** f____ **8** p____ **9** k____ **10** g____

2 Complete the table with the words from Exercise 1.

for food	for drink	things to put on food
	bottle	

3 Read the email. Who is at the café?

Hi Lara,

Thanks for your email. The concert sounds great! Can you send me photos of you and your brother at the concert? Thanks!

Well, I'm on holiday in Italy with my parents now. We're in Naples! I'm having a great time here. In the mornings we look at old buildings. Mum takes lots and lots of photos. She's really interested in old buildings. You can see them on my Instagram.

We eat pizza and ice cream for lunch every day – mmmm! In the afternoon, we go swimming because it's very hot here. I sometimes read, too. I've got lots of books with me!

I'm sitting in a café and I'm writing this email to you. My mum is talking to the waiter in Italian. (My mum teaches Italian at my school.) My brother's listening to music on his headphones. My dad's reading a book about the history of Italy.

What are you doing?

Write soon,

Beth

4 Read the email again. Answer the questions. Write sentences.

1 How often does Beth eat pizza?

2 When does she go swimming?

3 Where's Beth sitting?

4 Who's her mum talking to?

5 What's her brother doing?

6 What's her dad reading?

GRAMMAR — *can*: requests and permission

1 Match to make questions.

1	Can you clean	**a**	with my homework?
2	Can you put	**b**	football after school?
3	Can I use	**c**	the table, please?
4	Can you help me	**d**	bread and cheese for breakfast?
5	Can we go	**e**	the window, please?
6	Can we have	**f**	your smartphone, please?
7	Can we play	**g**	TV, please?
8	Can you show	**h**	me your new fitness tracker?
9	Can I watch	**i**	your books in your bag?
10	Can I open	**j**	to the park after school?

2 Read the questions. Is the person making a request or asking permission?

0 Can you clean the kitchen, please?
_____request_____

1 Can I have some chocolate, please?
_____

2 Can you close the window, please?
_____

3 Can you get me some milk from the shop, please?
_____

4 Can I have a table for two, please?
_____

5 Can I go to the park, please?
_____

3 Match the questions from Exercise 2 with these answers.

a Yes, of course. Be home for dinner, OK? ....

b Sure, no problem. Do you want some bread too? ....

c OK. Are you feeling cold? ....

d Oh, Dad! It's your turn to clean it. ___0___

e Yes, of course. Come this way, please. ....

f No, you can't eat it every day, Alba! ....

WRITING

1 Complete the conversation with the words in the box.

drink	eat	have	I	like
of	please	problem	water	

Waiter: Good afternoon.
Girl and boy: Hello!
Waiter: Would you like anything to
¹ _____?
Girl: Yes, please. Can I ² _____ a cheese sandwich please?
Waiter: Sure, no ³ _____. Would you ⁴ _____ a drink?
Girl: Yes, ⁵ _____. Can I have a glass of apple juice?
Waiter: Yes, ⁶ _____ course. And what can I get for you?
Boy: Um. Can ⁷ _____ have an egg sandwich, please?
Waiter: OK. Would you like a ⁸ _____ with that?
Girl: Yes, please. Can I have a glass of ⁹ _____.
Waiter: OK.

2 Look at the menu then write a conversation. Use the conversation in Exercise 1 to help you.

• MENU •

SANDWICHES
cheese
—
egg
—
chicken

DRINKS
juice
(orange/apple)
—
water
—
tea
—
coffee

HOT MEALS
pizza
—
tomato soup
—
chicken and rice

DESSERT
chocolate, vanilla
or strawberry
ice cream
—
fruit and
yoghurt

13 PLACES

VOCABULARY AND LISTENING

Places in a town

1 Look at the pictures. Complete the words.

1
2
3
4
5
6
7
8
9
10

1 h _____
2 p _____
3 m _____
4 r _____
5 b _____

6 u _____
7 c _____
8 s _____
9 s _____
10 h _____

2 Read the definitions. Write the words from Exercise 1.

1 You go here to watch a film. _____
2 You go here for a meal. _____
3 You go here to buy food. _____
4 You sleep here when you're on holiday. _____
5 You wait here for a train. _____
6 You go here to study after you leave school. _____
7 You go here to feel better. _____
8 You go here to play football and have picnics. _____
9 You go here to look at art. _____
10 You go here to get some money. _____

3 Where are the people? Write the words from Exercise 1.

1 Wow! These paintings are very old. _____
2 Can I have a room for two nights, please? _____
3 I haven't got any money! _____
4 Can I see a doctor? _____
5 When does the train to London leave? _____
6 Can I have a pizza, please? _____
7 What are you studying? _____
8 What time does the film start? _____
9 I need to buy some coffee and bread. _____
10 Let's sit next to the trees. _____

4 Listen to five conversations. Tick the words you hear.

bank ☐   museum ☐
university ☐ park ☐
cinema ☐   restaurant ☐
hospital ☐   school ☐
hotel ☐   supermarket ☐

5 Listen again. Complete the sentences with *There is* and *There isn't*.

1 _____ a bank on Tower Street.
2 _____ a park on Cambridge Road.
3 _____ a restaurant on Market Street.
4 _____ a café on Station Road.
5 _____ a museum on Long Street.
6 _____ a museum on Castle Street.
7 _____ a hotel on Green Road.

1 Complete the questions with *Is there a* or *Are there any*.

0 _____Is there a_____ bank in New Street?
1 _____ hotels in the town?
2 _____ swimming pool in Green Road?
3 _____ restaurants in Main Street?
4 _____ station in Park Road?

5 _____ football clubs in the town?
6 _____ park near Green Road?
7 _____ museum in Main Street?
8 _____ café in New Street?
9 _____ supermarkets in Green Road?
10 _____ bank in Park Road?

2 Look at the map. Answer the questions in Exercise 1. Write *Yes, there is*, *No, there isn't*, *Yes, there are* or *No, there aren't*.

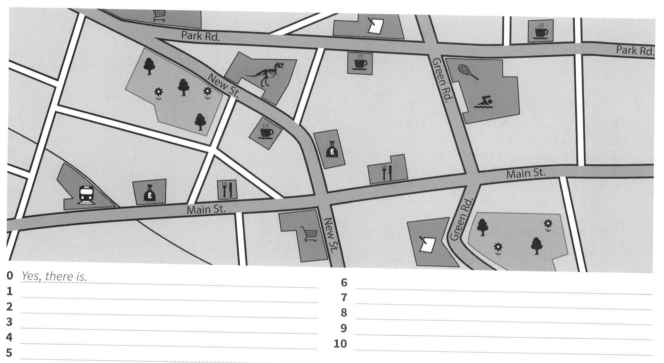

0 *Yes, there is.*
1 ....
2 ....
3 ....
4 ....
5 ....
6 ....
7 ....
8 ....
9 ....
10 ....

3 Complete the questions about where you live. Answer *Yes, there is. / Yes, there are.* or *No there isn't. / No, there aren't.*

1 _____ a university?

2 _____ a museum?

3 _____ any parks?

4 _____ a hospital?

5 _____ a swimming pool?

6 _____ any hotels?

7 _____ a train station?

8 _____ a cinema?

9 _____ any banks?

VOCABULARY AND READING

Adjectives: places

1 Match the adjectives with their opposites.

1 expensive   **a** tall
2 little   **b** interesting
3 boring   **c** cheap
4 short   **d** big

2 Circle four adjectives.

b	e	a	u	t	i	f	u	l
i	m	p	o	r	t	a	n	t
r	g	r	e	a	t	q	y	p
h	k	c	r	s	a	f	e	o

3 Choose the correct adjectives.

1 This film is *boring / interesting*. I like it.
2 Giraffes are very *tall / little* animals.
3 This phone is only £5 – that's very *cheap / expensive*.
4 This is a *great / boring* book. I don't like it.
5 Dad, I need a *old / new* bike. Can I have one for my birthday?

4 Read the descriptions. What is Arthur's Seat?

SANDRA, LONDON

I'm from Mexico, but I live in London now. London is a great place to live, but it's very expensive – you need lots of money to live here! There are lots of beautiful places in London. I like St Paul's Cathedral. It's an old building and very tall. Another place I like is Camden Market. It's an interesting part of the city. I go there every Sunday with my friends. We buy cheap clothes and enjoy the music in the street.

5 Read the texts again. Circle the adjectives.

6 Read the descriptions again. Write *Yes* or *No*. Correct the wrong sentences.

1 Sandra is from London.

2 Sandra thinks London isn't cheap.

3 Sandra goes to Camden Market on Saturdays.

4 Sanda never buys anything at Camden Market.

5 Mario isn't from Scotland.

6 Edinburgh castle is on a hill above the city.

7 Mario lives in a town.

8 Mario's sister works in a café.

9 Arthur's Seat is near Edinburgh centre.

MARIO, SCOTLAND

I'm from Italy, but I live in Edinburgh in Scotland. It's a beautiful city. I love Edinburgh Castle. It's on a hill above the city. It's very old! There are some good cafés near the castle. My mum works in one of them!

There's a great university in Edinburgh, lots of museums, shops and restaurants. And there is Arthur's Seat. It's a hill near the centre of the city. You can walk up it and see the whole of Edinburgh below you.

1 Look at the picture. Complete the sentences with the words in the box. Underline the prepositions.

cars	cat	~~girls~~	men	museum	pictures

0 There are two ___girls___ inside the café.
1 There's a _____ above the café.
2 There are some _____ inside the museum.
3 There are some _____ outside the station.
4 There's a _____ near the bus.
5 There are two _____ below the tall tree.

2 Look at the picture of Tom's house. Complete the sentences.

above	below	inside	near	outside

1 Tom's got two posters _____ his bed.
2 His desk is _____ the window.
3 The cat is _____ Tom's bedroom.
4 His desk is _____ his bed.
5 Tom is in his bedroom. He is _____ .

3 Choose the correct words.

1 It's hot. We're playing *inside / outside* the school.
2 We live *near / below* my grandparents. Our house is number 82 and theirs is number 86.
3 Wow! This is a very tall building. Look at the city *below / above*. The people look so small!
4 Look up! There's a plane flying *below / above* the city.

---

1 Hannah uses the adjective 'nice' five times in her description. Replace 'nice' with adjectives from this and other units.

My *favourite* place

My name is Hannah and I'm from Northern Ireland. I live in Madrid in Spain. I'm a student at the university. I study Spanish – it's a(n) [1] nice subject.

I like living in Madrid. It's a [2] nice city. My favourite place here is called El Retiro. This is a [3] nice park near the centre of the city. It's a [4] nice place to visit.

On sunny days, I like going to El Retiro with my friends. We sometimes go on the lake in a boat, but what I *really* like to do is have a picnic and talk to my friends. My friends are [5] nice.

1 _____ **4** _____
2 _____ **5** _____
3 _____

2 Read the text again. Answer the questions.

1 Where is Hannah from? _____
2 Where does she live? _____
3 What does she do? _____
4 What is her favourite subject? _____
5 What is her favourite place called? _____
6 What does she like doing there? _____

3 Write about your favourite place. Use the text in Exercise 1 to help you. Remember to use different adjectives.

VOCABULARY AND READING

Transport

1 Circle the odd word out.

0	car	(train)	taxi
1	coach	bus	plane
2	tram	boat	train
3	underground	bike	car
4	underground	tram	boat

2 Write the words from Exercise 1 under the pictures.

0 _train_

5 _____

1 _____

6 _____

2 _____

7 _____

3 _____

4 _____

9 _____

3 Read the text. Find four ways to travel around New York.

Transport in New York City

New York is full of life. People call it 'the city that never sleeps'. At all times of day, you see people walking to their offices, waiting for taxis, or going to the cinema, theatre and restaurants.

In a city like New York there are many ways to travel. One way is by underground. The New York underground is called 'the Subway'. It's got 27 lines and 472 stations – more than any other in the world! The Subway gets you around the city quickly, but it's very busy.

You can also travel around New York by one of the famous yellow taxis. Americans call these 'cabs'. Cabs are everywhere, but they can be expensive and you sometimes have to wait a long time for one.

Another way to travel in the city is by bike, but this isn't always safe because the roads are busy. If you think cycling around New York is too dangerous, then you can try the best way of getting around – on foot! Walking around New York City is a real adventure.

4 Read the text again. Answer the questions.

1 What do people call New York?

_____

2 What is the New York underground called?

_____

3 How many lines has it got?

_____

4 How many stations has it got?

_____

5 What colour are the taxis in New York?

_____

6 What are taxis called in New York?

_____

7 Which is the best way of getting around the city?

_____

because, and, but, or

1 Write sentences with *because*.

0 Magda's mum / drink lots of water / it / be good for her
Magda's mum drinks lots of water because it's good for her.

1 Laura / play football with her friends / she / like it

2 Sophie / leave home at 8.30 / the bus leave at 8.40

3 Martin / take great photos / he / have got a new camera

4 Janina / do her homework every day / she / be a good student

5 Gina / make a sandwich / she / be hungry

6 Maddie / be at the concert / she / like the singer

7 I / walk to school / I / not like catch / the bus

8 My sister / go swimming every day / she / enjoy it

2 Choose the correct words.

1 We can go to the swimming pool *and / or / but* the shopping centre. We haven't got time to go swimming and shopping.

2 My brother would like to go the park *and / or / but* my sister wants to see the castle.

3 After school, I do my homework *and / or / but* talk to my friends online.

4 Sam wants to go the cinema *and / or / but* he isn't feeling very well.

5 Lily, do you want a cheese *and / or / but* a chicken sandwich?

6 I'd like a cheese and tomato pizza please *and / or / but* a glass of water.

7 It's OK, we've got time to go the museum *and / or / but* the concert!

8 My brother's got a smartphone *and / or / but* I haven't got one. I think they're boring.

9 Would you like a glass of apple juice *and / or / but* orange juice?

3 Complete the text with *because, and, but* or *or*.

Hello everyone! It's a beautiful day in the city. Today I'm in London with my friends: Toni, Angelo, Bea ¹_____ Katie. Ali isn't here ²_____ she isn't feeling very well. We're taking lots of photos!

Bea ³_____ Toni have got great digital cameras, ⁴_____ I'm using my smartphone! This is a photo of Big Ben!

Angelo says we've got time to do one more thing before we have to catch our train back to Brighton. We can go to the Tate Modern museum ⁵_____ the British Museum, ⁶_____ I want to go to the Tate Modern museum ⁷_____ the British Museum! Hmm, where shall we go?

Phrases: going out

1 Look at the pictures. Complete the text with the words in the box.

famous person	dad	film	museum	friends	~~park~~
restaurant	running	shopping	six o'clock	swimming	

My name's Michelle. After school I sometimes go to the **0** _____park_____ with my friend, Sasha. But we never go **1** _____ because I don't like the water. I often meet my **2** _____ at **3** _____ on Friday evening and we go **4** _____. He's really fast! At the weekends, I sometimes visit a **5** _____ or I go **6** _____ with my parents and we go to a **7** _____ for lunch. I always take my camera because I want to meet a **8** _____! In the evening I go out with my **9** _____. We often go to the cinema to see a **10** _____.

2 Complete the table with vocabulary from Exercise 1. Some words and phrases can go in more than one place.

go	
go out with	
go to	*the park*
meet	
visit	
see	

3 Listen to Will's conversations with four friends. Who is in hospital? Who doesn't like tennis?

4 Listen again. Look at Will's diary. Tick the right answer.

	Saturday		Sunday	
am	play football in the park	✓	go swimming	☐
	go to the museum	☐	play tennis	☐
pm	go shopping	☐	go to the cinema	☐
	visit Marta	☐	go to a concert	☐

5 Listen again. Complete the sentences.

	Saturday	Sunday
am	Meet James outside the park at **1**_____ o'clock.	Meet Freddie in the **4**_____ near the **5**_____ at **6**_____ o'clock.
pm	Meet Emily outside the **2**_____ at **3**_____ o'clock.	Meet Beth outside the **7**_____ at **8**_____.

1   **Match to make conversations.**

1   Let's play football tomorrow morning!
2   Shall we go swimming after school?
3   Let's go to the cinema this afternoon!
4   Let's go to London on Saturday morning!
5   Shall we go shopping tomorrow?
6   Shall we go to the museum this afternoon?

a   Sorry, I can't. I've got an important tennis match. It starts at four o'clock.
b   Yes, that's a good idea. I've got a new ball!
c   Sorry, I can't. I've got to visit my grandparents in Scotland.
d   Yes, that's a good idea. I'd like to see the new paintings.
e   Yes, that's a good idea. Let's buy some clothes.
f   I'd love to. I want to see the new Batman film.

2   **Complete the conversations with *Let's* or *Shall we*.**

Tom: ¹ _____ meet after school on Friday. We can go swimming.
Liam: Sorry, I can't on Friday. ² _____ go on Saturday morning?
Tom: OK!
Ana: ³ _____ have lunch in the café tomorrow?
Maria: I'd love to!
Ana: ⁴ _____ meet outside the station at 12.00.
Maria: Great! See you tomorrow!
Hasan: I'm bored!
Jon: ⁵ _____ go to the cinema?
Hasan: That's a good idea! ⁶ _____ go to the new one next to the museum.
Jon: Sure.

3   **Complete the conversation with the words in the box.**

| can't   good idea   let's |
| let's meet   shall we |

Liu: ¹ _____ go to the café after school.
Valeria: Sorry, I ² _____ . I've got English club.
Liu: OK. ³ _____ go shopping on Saturday?
Valeria: Yes, that's a ⁴ _____ . I want to buy some new jeans!
Liu: Great! ⁵ _____ at 10.30 outside the station.
Valeria: OK. See you there!

1   **Read the text. Answer the questions.**

My
WEEKENDS
by Mia Wilson

I love the weekend! It's my favourite time of the week because I don't have to go to school. I do a lot of things with my friends at weekends. We have lunch in a café on Saturdays. We go shopping or go to a museum in the afternoon. And we sometimes like going to concerts or the cinema on Saturday evenings.

But the weekend isn't all about my friends. It's a very important time for my family, too. On Saturday mornings we all have breakfast together. We talk about the week and our plans for the weekend. Dad makes pancakes and everyone loves them!

On Sundays we always go out for lunch to a nice restaurant in town. We usually go to an Italian place, but sometimes we try somewhere different. I enjoy these lunches with my family.

On Sunday evenings we often sit down together in the living room and watch a film. It can take a long time to choose a film! Dad likes films that make him laugh, Mum likes films about history and my brother and I prefer films about science and life in the future!

1   When does Mia go to museums with her friends?

2   What does Mia like doing on Saturday evenings?

3   What does Mia's family eat for breakfast on Saturday mornings?

4   Does Mia's family always eat at the same Italian restaurant on Sundays?

5   What does Mia's family do on Sunday evenings?

2   **Write about your family's weekend. Use the text in Exercise 1 to help you.**

VOCABULARY AND LISTENING

Clothes

1 Put the letters in the right order to make clothes words.

1 ehso ....

6 aejsn ....

2 sithr-T ....

7 tekjca ....

3 slaessg ....

8 rikts ....

4 sesrd ....

9 sserruot ....

5 riths ....

2 Read the sentences. What is the word?

1 You wear this to tell the time. ....
2 You wear these to help you see. ....
3 You wear these on your feet. ....
4 These are trousers. They are usually blue or black. ....
5 You wear this over a T-shirt or shirt. ....
6 You wear this with jeans or in summer. ....
7 Girls wear this. It covers the body and legs. ....

3 What are you wearing today? Write sentences. Use words from Exercise 1.

I'm wearing a blue T-shirt and black jeans.
....
....
....
....

4 Listen to some students talking about the clothes they wear to school. Who loves wearing T-shirts?

5 Listen again. Match the students to the photos. Write *Maria*, *Jack*, *Lisa* and *Tom*.

1 ....

3 ....

2 ....

4 ....

6 Listen again. Write *Yes* or *No.* Correct the wrong sentences.

1 Maria doesn't like wearing skirts.

2 Jack wears a black jumper to school.

3 Jack likes the colour grey.

4 Lisa wears a skirt or dress to school.

5 Lisa plays football.

6 Tom isn't wearing his glasses now.

7 Tom doesn't like wearing shorts.

GRAMMAR Plurals: spelling

1 Look at the plurals. Circle the plural which is different.

0	shoes	(boxes)	doctors	girls
1	glasses	watches	sandwiches	hotels
2	dresses	cakes	girls	waiters
3	cinemas	pencils	parties	teachers
4	dictionaries	factories	jeans	universities
5	jeans	trousers	clothes	cakes

2 Complete the table. Use the words from Exercise 1.

always plural	add -s	add -es	change -y to -ies
clothes	*coats*	*addresses*	*bodies*

3 Complete the sentences with the plural form of the word in brackets.

1 Have you got any black _____ (T-shirt).
2 Mum's buying some _____ (book) to take on our holiday.
3 Sam's got two sisters. They're _____ (baby).
4 I need to buy some new _____ (clothes).
5 Look at these beautiful old _____ (house).
6 Please write your _____ (address) on the forms.
7 Do you know what I love doing? Watching _____ (film)!
8 Mum, where are my blue _____ (skirt)?
9 There are lots of new _____ (shop) in our town.
10 Do you have any digital _____ (watch)?
11 We've got three _____ (computer) in our house.

Phrases: people

1 **Match the opposites.**

1	tall	**a**	old
2	short hair	**b**	short
3	young	**c**	fat
4	slim	**d**	long hair

2 **Choose the correct phrases.**

1 She's got *beautiful eyes / long hair*.
2 He's got *dark hair / a red nose*.
3 She's got *short hair / long hair*.
4 He's got *a red nose / long hair*.
5 He's got *a brown beard / a grey beard*.
6 He's got *a red nose / big ears*.

3 **Read the blog. Who is visiting Stanley this week?**

Hello, my name is Stanley. I'm taking lots of photos at the moment because I go to a camera club. This is a photograph of the park near our house. We often go to this park on Sunday afternoons.

This week, my grandparents are visiting us, so there are more of us in the park than usual. It's a very cold day today. Everyone's wearing very warm clothes!

OK. Let me tell you about my family at the park. My dad is wearing gloves and coat. My dad's got quite long hair. My mum's got beautiful, short hair. She's wearing her favourite winter coat.

My grandmother and grandfather are standing behind my sister. My grandfather is wearing gloves and a jacket. My grandmother is wearing gloves and a beautiful coat.

My brother is wearing jeans and a jacket. My sister is standing next to my brother. She's wearing a jacket, but she isn't wearing gloves. 'I don't think it's very cold!' she says.

4 **Read the text. Complete the table with what the people are wearing.**

Stanley's dad	
Stanley's mum	
Stanley's grandmother	
Stanley's grandfather	
Stanley's brother	
Stanley's sister	

5 **Read the text again. Answer the questions.**

1 Why is Stanley taking lots of photos?

2 Where are the family?

3 Why are there more people in the park than usual?

4 Who thinks it isn't very cold?

5 Who has got long hair?

6 Why is everyone wearing warm clothes?

1 Make sentences about Arthur and Florence.

Arthur	is	a black beard.
	has got	short.
	is wearing	glasses.
Florence	is	dark hair.
	has got	a long skirt.
	is wearing	tall.

2 Rewrite the sentences with *is* or *has*.

0 Pablo's tall.
   Pablo is tall.

1 Lee's got short hair.

2 Julia's wearing purple shoes.

3 Robbie's got blue eyes.

4 Laura's beautiful.

5 Mathew's wearing a grey jacket.

3 Look at the pictures of Roberto and Alesandra and write sentences. Use the words in the box.

| dark eyes | glasses | long hair |
| short hair | slim | young |

Roberto's ....
He's ....
He's got ....
He's got ....

Alesandra's got ....
She's ....

1 Read the descriptions. Match the descriptions to the people.

1 Daniel's from Brazil. He's tall and he's got short black hair. Today he's wearing short and a T-shirt. He isn't wearing glasses. Daniel's got a football match in the park. ....

2 Nadia is from Russia. She's got long hairs and she's wearing a skirts and a jacket. Today is her first day at her new school so her mum is taking a photo of her. ....

3 David from Spain. He's got long hair. He's wearing jean and a T-shirt. He's wearing glass too. It's his birthday today. I can't wait to go to his party. ....

4 Ashen's Turkish. She's got long hair. She's wearing a jeans and a jacket. She never wears a watches. Ashen's got a concert tonight! She plays the piano. ....

2 Read the texts again. Circle six mistakes. Correct the mistakes.

1 ....
2 ....
3 ....
4 ....
5 ....
6 ....

3 Write a description of someone in your family or a friend. Use the descriptions in Exercise 1 to help you.

16 BUY IT!

VOCABULARY AND LISTENING

Shopping

1 **Match the words with the definitions.**

1	diary	**a**	You find this in a pencil case.
2	scissors	**b**	You can colour a picture with this.
3	umbrella	**c**	You can cut these and give them to someone on their birthday.
4	toothbrush		
5	rucksack	**d**	You can eat these.
6	flowers	**e**	You play this with your friends.
7	sweets	**f**	You use this when it rains.
8	paint	**g**	These grow in the garden.
9	plants	**h**	You put your things in here for school.
10	rubber	**i**	You use these to send letters.
11	stamps	**j**	You cut things with these.
12	game	**k**	You write in this every day.
		l	You clean your teeth with this.

2 **Complete the sentences. Use some of the words from Exercise 1.**

1 What _____ can we play?
2 These _____ aren't very good. I can't cut the paper with them.
3 Where's my _____? I have to brush my teeth.
4 Oh, look – it's raining! Where's my _____?
5 I never eat chocolate, cake or _____. I don't like sugar.
6 Does this _____ have red or white flowers?
7 Lisa is good at art and she wants some new _____.

🔊 18 **3** **Listen to the conversation between Zoe and her dad. Where are Zoe and her family going?**

🔊 18 **4** **Listen again. Match the people to the objects.**

1	Zoe's brother	**a**	books
2	Zoe's sister	**b**	sweets
3	Zoe's mum	**c**	paints
4	Zoe's dad	**d**	toothbrush

🔊 18 **5** **Listen again. Who says these words? Write _D_ for Dad and _Z_ for Zoe.**

1 Have we got everything? ....
2 He can't find his old one. ....
3 I'd like to get an umbrella. ....
4 That's true. ....
5 Say it again, please. ....
6 Do you need anything? ....
7 I think I've got everything. ....

1 Put the words in the right order to make sentences.

1 need / sleep / I / to / go / to

2 friends / to / to / New York / go / My / want

3 my / homework / need / do / I / to

4 buy / needs / Dad / dinner / food / to / for

5 want / party / big / birthday / a / I

6 need / buy / holiday / We / the / some / for / to / clothes

7 want / basketball / play / to / I

2 Match the sentences with the pictures.

1 He wants to go to the park.
2 She needs to clean her room.
3 He wants an ice cream.
4 She needs a drink.
5 He needs to buy a new ball.
6 She wants to be famous.

3 Choose the correct words to complete the sentences.

1 I *need* / *want* to go to the swimming pool tomorrow.
2 Mari is doing an exam. She *needs* / *wants* a blue pen.
3 It's my birthday tomorrow. I *need* / *want* to have a party.
4 We haven't got any food. We *need* / *want* to go shopping.
5 My mum likes music. She *needs* / *wants* to go to the concert at the weekend.
6 Nina thinks Mexico is a beautiful country. She *needs* / *wants* to visit it.

4 Correct the sentences.

1 My dad wanting to buy some shoes.

2 I want watch a film on Saturday.

3 I needs to go to sleep.

4 My brother want to play football for Barcelona.

5 I'm hungry. I need to eating something.

6 My sister needs study for her English test.

7 Mum wants to goes to the beach.

5 Complete the sentences. Use the correct form of *need* / *needs* or *want* / *wants*.

1 **A:** Leo, Lana _____ to come to your party.
   B: Great!

2 **A:** Let's have a picnic in the park!
   B: OK, but we _____ to buy some food!

3 **A:** Cathy's tired.
   B: She _____ to go to bed.

4 **A:** Why is Rachel learning Turkish?
   B: Because she _____ to go to Istanbul in July.

5 **A:** I _____ to go to their concert in July!
   B: Me too! I love that band!

6 **A:** Mum, your bike is very dirty!
   B: I know. I _____ to clean it.

7 **A:** Do you _____ to go to the cinema?
   B: Sorry, I can't! It's my dad's birthday.

VOCABULARY AND READING

Money and prices

1 Choose the correct words.

1 € dollar / euro
2 £ pound / cent
3 p euro / pence
4 $ dollar / pound
5 c cent / pence

2 Write the prices.

0 €4.10   *four euros ten cents*
1 £8.50   ....
2 70c   ....
3 €30   ....
4 £9.20   ....
5 $6   ....
6 €8.25   ....
7 15p   ....
8 $12.40   ....
9 10c   ....
10 £1.60   ....

3 Look at the pictures. Write the price of the objects.

£2.50

€7.00

$2.15

$5.00

€9.00

1 The sandwich is ....
2 The plate is ....
3 The ball is ....
4 The bag is ....
5 The car is ....

4 Read the conversations. Match the photos to the conversations.

 A
 B
 C
 D

1 ....
Assistant: Good morning. Can I help you?
Emma: Good morning. I'd like some flowers, please.
Assistant: Sure. Do you like these big pink ones?
Emma: Not really, I think they're too expensive.
Assistant: OK.
Emma: But I love these small white flowers.
Assistant: They're £4.25.
Emma: Great!

2 ....
Assistant: Can I help you?
Henry: Yes. I need a birthday present for my brother.
Assistant: I see. How old is he?
Henry: He's five years old.
Assistant: What about paints?
Henry: He's got lots of paints. He likes playing. Have you got any games?
Assistant: Oh, yes. We've got lots of them over here.

3 ....
Lucy: This is my favourite shop, Mum!
Mum: Yes. Look at these beautiful dresses!
Lucy: I need a new dress for Tom's party. Do you like this one, Mum?
Mum: No. It's too short.
Lucy: Do you like this long one?
Mum: Yes, I do!

4 ....
Mum: Let's go to the café.
Jack: Good idea! Can I have a cake?
Mum: Sure. What do you want to drink?
Jack: Some orange juice, please.
Mum: OK. I'll have some coffee. Where's the waiter?
Jack: He's by the door, Mum.

5 Read the conversations again. Are the sentences right (✓) or wrong (✗)?

1 Emma thinks the white flowers are too expensive.
2 The white flowers are £4.25.
3 Henry's brother hasn't got any paints.
4 Henry wants to buy a game.
5 Lucy needs a dress for her holiday.
6 Lucy's mum likes the long dress.
7 Jack's mum would like some coffee.

1 Choose the correct words to complete the sentences.

1 Martin can't ride his little brother's bike. He's too *short / tall.*
2 Lisa doesn't want to walk home. She's too *old / tired.*
3 Tom can't do his homework. It's too *difficult / easy!*
4 Helen likes the shoes, but they're €300! That's too *cheap / expensive.*
5 Can I have some cold water in my tea? It's too *cold / hot.*
6 My brother can't drive a car. He's too *old / young.*
7 My little brother's shoes are too *big / small* for him. He needs some new ones.
8 We're having a great holiday, but it's too *long / short* – only five days!
9 Where's your new T-shirt? That one's too *clean / dirty!*

2 Complete the conversations. Use *too* + an adjective from Exercise 1.

0 **A:** We never go to the River Café.
B: Why not?
A: It's ____*too expensive*____. A pizza is €15.00!

1 **A:** Let's play tennis.
B: I can't. I'm _____. I need to go to bed.

2 **A:** Hugo only likes hot food.
B: Doesn't he like ice cream?
A: No, he doesn't! He says it's
_____.

3 **A:** Does your little sister go to school?
B: No, she doesn't. She's
_____. She's only three.

4 **A:** Do you like basketball?
B: Yes, I do, but I'm _____ to play it.

5 **A:** Why don't you wear your blue shirt to the party?
B: I can't. It's _____. I need to wash it.

6 **A:** My grandfather doesn't want to come to the park.
B: Why not?
A: Well, he's 70 years old. He says he's
_____ to play football.

1 Put the conversation in the right order.

A Yes? Can I help you? ....
B Excuse me. ___*1*___
C Great! Can I have that one? ....
D Here you are. ....
E It's £25. ....
F Oh, that's too expensive. How much is the brown one? ....
G Sure. That's £15, please. ....
H Thanks. Bye. ....
J The brown one's £15. ....
K Yes. I need a new rucksack. I like the red one. How much is it? ....

2 Look at the photo. Write a shopping conversation. Use the conversation in Exercise 1 and the phrases in the box to help you.

Can I help you?	Do you like this/these?
Excuse me.	Here you are.
How much …?	I need some/a …
It's/They're …	Sorry. This is / These are too …
Yes, of course.	

VOCABULARY AND LISTENING

The natural world

1 Match the descriptions to the pictures.

1 There's a **river** in the **forest**.
2 In this **garden** there is **grass**, and there are **trees** and **flowers**.
3 Here we can see the **sea** and the **beach**.
4 This is the **countryside** near my home.

2 Complete the sentences with the words in bold from Exercise 1.

1 Which do you prefer: swimming in the _____ or in a river?
2 Dad, we need to cut the _____! It's very long.
3 There is a _____ near my grandparents' house, but it's not sandy, it's full of stones.
4 My grandparents love their _____. It's behind their house. In the summer they spend all their time there. It's got lots of unusual flowers.
5 We've got lots of tall _____ in our garden. My brother and sister love climbing them!
6 I like living in a city, but my uncle and aunt prefer the _____. There are no tall buildings where they live and there aren't many cars.
7 The Amazon is a special type of _____. There are more trees and it rains a lot.
8 I'd like to go on holiday to Egypt. I want to go on a boat on the Nile! Do you know the Nile? It's a very long _____.
9 Let's buy Mum some _____ for her birthday! She likes them.

3 Listen to the conversation. Where is Jack? Why is he there?

4 Listen again. Which sentence is right (✓)?

1 Jack is in the UK. ☐
Jack is in Canada. ☐
2 Jack is with his family. ☐
Jack isn't with his family. ☐
3 Jack's grandmother is 50 tomorrow. ☐
Jack's grandmother is 60 tomorrow. ☐
4 Jack's grandmother lives in Canada. ☐
Jack's grandmother doesn't live in Canada. ☐
5 Jack's hotel is near a forest. ☐
Jack's hotel is in a forest. ☐
6 Jack's father enjoys walking by the river. ☐
Jack's mother enjoys walking by the river. ☐
7 Ava can meet Jack on Sunday. ☐
Ava can't meet Jack on Sunday. ☐

1 Complete the table with the comparative form of the adjectives in the box.

clean	dirty	easy	fat	hot	long	new	nice	~~sad~~	tall

+ er	+ r	double letter + er	y → i + er
		sadder	

2 Complete the sentences with the comparative form of the adjectives.

1 Our English classroom is _____ (big) than our music classroom.
2 Paris is _____ (cold) than Seville.
3 Linda is _____ (happy) on Friday than on Monday.
4 My grandparents' house is _____ (old) than our house.
5 My brother is always _____ (hungry) than his friends!
6 My sister is a _____ (fast) runner than I am.
7 The sea in Spain is _____ (warm) than the sea in Scotland.
8 I am _____ (young) than most of my friends.
9 I am _____ (short) than you.

3 Write sentences.

0 Hugo's teacher / Eleanor's teacher (old)
Hugo's teacher is older than Eleanor's teacher.
1 English / Chinese (easy)

2 Mexico / Russia (hot)

3 a bus / a taxi (long)

4 a car / a school bus (fast)

5 orange juice / tea (nice)

6 London / Madrid (big)

7 winter / summer (cold)

8 my sister / my brother (young)

4 Look at the pictures. Read the sentences. Write *Yes* or *No*.

0 Tom is shorter than Karen.
    No
1 Tom' hair is longer than Karen's.

2 Tom's cat is fatter than Karen's cat.

3 Tom's garden is nicer than Karen's garden.

4 Tom's face is dirtier than Karen's face.

5 Compare the boy and girl. Write six comparative sentences using the words in the box.

happy	old	short	sad	tall	young

1 _____
2 _____
3 _____
4 _____
5 _____
6 _____

Adjectives: opinions

1 Complete the adjectives.

1 p _ p _ l _ r
2 _ m _ z _ ng
3 f _ nt _ st _ c
4 _ ttr _ ct _ v _
5 _ n _ s _ _ l
6 w _ nd _ _ f u _

2 Match the adjectives in Exercise 1 with the definitions below.

a Something or someone that is different in some way. ....
b When something is very, very good we can use these three words to describe it. ....
c This means that something or someone is nice to look at. ....
d Someone or something that everyone likes. ....

3 Read the email. Match the words in bold in the text with the pictures.

1 ....   2 ....   3 ....

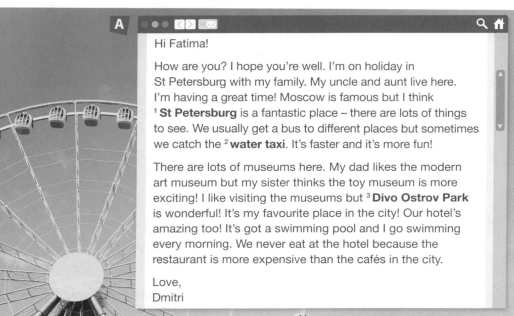

A

Hi Fatima!

How are you? I hope you're well. I'm on holiday in St Petersburg with my family. My uncle and aunt live here. I'm having a great time! Moscow is famous but I think ¹ **St Petersburg** is a fantastic place – there are lots of things to see. We usually get a bus to different places but sometimes we catch the ² **water taxi**. It's faster and it's more fun!

There are lots of museums here. My dad likes the modern art museum but my sister thinks the toy museum is more exciting! I like visiting the museums but ³ **Divo Ostrov Park** is wonderful! It's my favourite place in the city! Our hotel's amazing too! It's got a swimming pool and I go swimming every morning. We never eat at the hotel because the restaurant is more expensive than the cafés in the city.

Love,
Dmitri

B

C

4 Read the email again. Complete the sentences.

1 Dimitri is on holiday with his _____.
2 Dimitri's _____ and _____ live in St Petersburg.
3 Dimitri is travelling around the city by water taxi and _____.
4 Dimitri's _____ likes the modern art museum.
5 Dimitri's _____ likes the toy museum.
6 Dimitri says Divo Ostrov Park is _____.

5 Read the email again. Answer the questions.

1 How does Dimitri describe St Petersburg?

2 Why does he like catching the water taxi?

3 Are there many museums in St Petersburg?

4 What's Dimitri's favourite place?

5 When does Dimitri go swimming?

6 Why doesn't Dimitri's family eat at the restaurant in the hotel?

GRAMMAR Comparatives: long adjectives

1 Write sentences. Use comparative adjectives.

1 the beach / fun / a museum

2 films / exciting / books

3 science / difficult / geography

4 Messi / famous / my dad

5 a pizza / expensive / sandwich

6 homework / important / computer games

7 jackets / expensive / hats

2 Write five sentences with comparative adjectives. Use the words in the box.

a car / a house	basketball / tennis
history / maths	London / my town/city
Russian / English	summer / winter

0 *I think tennis is more popular than basketball.*

1 ....

2 ....

3 ....

4 ....

5 ....

WRITING

1 Match the answers with the questions.

1 What is your favourite place to visit?

2 Where is it?

3 What do you like about it?

4 What do you like to do there?

5 When is the best time to visit?

a It's in a part of Wales called Pembrokeshire.

b I like the amazing beaches and the old castle.

c The summer! There are lots of people there then.

d A town called Tenby.

e I like playing football on the beach and swimming in the sea.

---

2 Read the text about Tenby. Find and correct six spelling mistakes.

MY FAVOURITE PLACE TO VISIT

WHERE IS IT?

My favourite place is called Tenby. It's a small town by the sea. It's in a wunderful part of Wales called Pembrokeshire. Tenby is near the town of Carmarthen – I live there with my parents and my sister.

WHY I LIKE IT

My grandparents live in Tenby in Wales and we often visit them at weekends. In the summer we go almost every weekend! I like Tenby becuse it's got amazing beaches and an old castle looking out to the sea.

WHAT I LIKE DOING THERE

My favourite thing is going down to the beech and playing football. I like swiming in the sea too, but the sea can be quite cold! The other thing I like to do is go out on a boat on the sea around the town. We go to Caldey Island near Tenby. We sometimes see seals there!

WHEN I LIKE TO VISIT

I visit Tenby every year. The best time to go is the summer. Tenby is poplar in the summer. There are always lots of people in the town and they are hapy and enjoy themselves.

3 Answer the questions in Exercise 1 so that they are true for you.

1 ....

2 ....

3 ....

4 ....

5 ....

4 Write about your favourite place to visit. Use the text in Exercise 2 and your answers from Exercise 3 to help you.

VOCABULARY AND READING

Weather

1 Find 11 weather and season words.

a	x	j	w	i	k	o	s
u	f	r	i	q	p	a	u
t	w	a	n	y	d	f	m
u	a	i	t	h	o	t	m
m	r	n	e	g	r	t	e
n	m	u	r	a	c	z	r
s	n	o	w	c	o	l	d
s	p	r	i	n	g	v	b
w	i	n	d	l	s	u	n

2 Complete the sentences with words from Exercise 1.

1 It's very _____ today. It's 0° outside!
2 I live in Siberia. In the _____ we all wear big coats.
3 We can't go to the park today – the _____ is too strong.
4 I don't like cold weather but I like _____ weather.
5 Look at the _____. Our garden's white!
6 I like _____. After a cold winter, it's great to wear a T-shirt again.
7 Look at the _____. Have we got an umbrella?
8 My mum's sitting in the garden. It's hot today and she likes to sit in the _____ .

3 Read the message board. Where is it cold today?

WEATHER | THE SEASONS | WEATHER FORECASTS | YOUR PHOTO

Weather chat

QUESTION: **WHAT'S THE WEATHER LIKE WHERE YOU LIVE?**

Hi, I'm Tomas and I'm in Mexico City. I usually play outside because it's hot here but I'm playing board games in the house today because it's raining.
Tomas

Hi. I live in São Paulo in Brazil. It's very hot today. I like summer because I often go swimming with my friends. I love swimming in the sea.
Ana

Hello. My name's David. I'm from Tarifa in Spain. It's warm here today but there's a lot of wind – there's always a lot of wind in my town because it's near the sea.
David

Hi. I'm Eva and I'm from Moscow. It's winter here and you need a big coat in Moscow in winter! It's very cold and today it's snowing, too!
Eva

Hello, I'm from Turkey! My name's Adem and I live in Ankara. I want to go to the cinema today because it's raining.
Adem

Hi. I'm Isabella. I live in Venice. It often rains here in winter but it isn't raining today. It isn't very warm – it's cold. I like the cold in winter. Winter is my favourite time of the year in Venice.
Isabella

4 Read the message board again. Answer the questions.

1 Who goes swimming with her friends in the summer?
2 Who wants to go to the cinema?
3 Where does it often rain in winter?
4 Where is it snowing today?
5 Who lives in Mexico City?
6 Who lives where there is a lot of wind?

1 Match to make sentences.

1 Henry doesn't like winter because

2 I'd like to buy this jacket but

3 Alberto wants to go to the beach because

4 I like studying Chinese but

5 Magda's hair is wet because

6 Meg's hat and jacket are white because

a it's cold.
b it's snowing.
c it's too expensive.
d it's a hot day.
e it's very hard.
f it's raining.

2 Rewrite the underlined sentences with *it* or *it's*.

0 Giovanni loves art. <u>Art is fun.</u>
It's fun.

1 Carla always watches tennis on TV.
<u>Henry thinks tennis is boring.</u>

2 Adam eats ice cream in the summer.
<u>His sister doesn't like ice cream.</u>

3 Pep and Javier often play football.
<u>They aren't very good at football.</u>

4 Sophie lives in Manchester.
<u>Manchester is a big city in Britain.</u>

5 **A:** Can Carmen speak English?
B: <u>Yes, she's good at English.</u>

6 This is one of Stanley's photographs.
<u>Would you like to look at the photograph?</u>

7 I've got a piano. <u>I can't play the piano very well.</u>

8 Paula lives in Colombia. <u>Colombia is in South America.</u>

9 Eliot is from the USA. <u>The USA is a very big country.</u>

10 Amber goes running. <u>She's likes running.</u>

3 Complete the dialogue with *it* or *it's*.

George: Hi, Florence!

Florence: Hi, George! How are you?

George: I'm OK, thanks. And you?

Florence: I'm fine too. ⁰*It's a nice day today.*

George: Yes, it is. ¹_____ very sunny! Shall we go to the park?

Florence: Oh, I don't know, George. ²_____ very hot. Can't we go to the cinema?

George: The cinema? I don't want to stay inside on a day like this.

Florence: There's a nice café near the cinema. We can go there.

George: Where is ³_____?

Florence: ⁴_____ opposite the cinema, next to the clothes shop. I'll send you a photo.

George: Oh, yes, I know ⁵_____! ⁶_____ a great place! I sometimes go there with my brother.

Florence: Would you like to go today?

George: OK!

4 Correct the underlined sentences.

0 <u>It very cold today.</u> I don't want to go out.
It's very cold today.

1 I like chocolate. <u>But I don't eat it's every day.</u>

2 I know where your camera is! <u>It on the table in the kitchen.</u>

3 I like singing. <u>But I'm not very good at it's.</u>

4 <u>It a beautiful day today.</u> Let's go to the park.

5 This is my new phone. <u>It great!</u>

VOCABULARY AND LISTENING

Holidays

1 Put the letters in the right order to make travel verbs.

1 lyf ....
2 gte ....
3 eocm ....
4 ayst ....
5 tahcc ....

6 evdir ....
7 iitvs ....
8 eavle ....
9 veltar ....

2 Read the sentences. What is the word?

1 This is a verb. It means to move through the air in a plane.

....

2 This is a verb. It means to move on a road in a car, lorry or bus.

....

3 This is a verb. It means to go on a journey by something like a plane, car or bus.

....

4 This is a verb. It means to go away from a place forever or for a short time.

....

5 This is a noun. It's a place where you can stay when you are on holiday.

....

6 This is a noun. It's a place you can sleep in on holiday. We usually put it in a field.

....

3 Listen to the conversation. Match the people with the photographs.

1 Katie ....

2 Tom ....

3 Mel ....

4 Listen again. Complete the sentences with *Tom*, *Ed*, *Katie* or *Mel*.

1 .... wants to be in a different country.
2 .... is on holiday for two weeks.
3 .... goes dancing every night.
4 .... is staying in a tent.
5 .... isn't going away this year.
6 .... is going to stay with her grandparents.

GRAMMAR   Prepositions: *with, for, until*

1 Choose the correct words to complete the sentences.

1 Ethan's tired. He needs to go to bed *for / with* a couple of hours.
2 Olivia and Alex want to stay in the park *with / until* seven o'clock because they haven't got school tomorrow.
3 Abigail can't come to my party because she's on holiday *for / until* ten days.
4 My friend Sam's in France *for / until* next Monday.
5 Do you like going to museums *with / until* your friends?
6 Isabelle plays tennis *for / until* an hour every day after school.
7 Zach's staying with us *until / with* next week.
8 Would you like to come *with / for* me to the concert on Saturday?
9 Emily can't play tennis *for / with* Hannah today because it's raining.

2 Complete the email with *for, with* or *until*.

> Hi Aunt Jules!
>
> I'm on holiday in Cornwall ¹_____ ten days ²_____ my friends from school. What a beautiful place! We're staying in St. Ives. Today we want to visit Tintagel Castle. We're having a great time and we don't go home ³_____ next Saturday! I'm sleeping in a tent ⁴_____ Veronica and Holly. I'm very tired because we talk ⁵_____ hours every night. We don't go to sleep ⁶_____ 11 o'clock!
>
> Love Natasha x

3 Read the email again. Answer the questions.

1 Where is Natasha?
2 Who is she with?
3 Where is she staying?
4 What does she want to visit today?
5 Where is she sleeping?
6 Why is she tired?

WRITING

1 Read the postcard and answer the questions.

> Hi Ross,
> I'm on holiday with my parents in Florence in Italy. We're here until Sunday. It's sunny today but it isn't very hot. I love it here. There are lots of interesting places to visit and great restaurants too. Our hotel is near the shops and I go shopping for an hour every day. Today, we're visiting a famous museum called the Uffizi Gallery. I'm writing this postcard in the museum's café.
>
> Love from Jess xx

1 Where is Jess?
2 Who is Jess with?
3 What is the weather like today?
4 What is Jess doing today?

2 Imagine you are on holiday. Answer the questions.

1 Where are you?
2 Who are you with?
3 What is the weather like today?
4 What are you doing?

3 Write a postcard to a friend. Use the text in Exercise 1 and your answers from Exercises 1 and 2 to help you.

19 A FANTASTIC CONCERT

VOCABULARY AND LISTENING

Adjectives (1)

1 Put the letters in the right order to make adjectives.

1 dlou   _____
2 oslw   _____
3 eatl   _____
4 seya   _____
5 staf   _____
6 idfrlnye   _____
7 ceeidtx   _____
8 iiuftlcdf   _____

2 Complete the sentences with the adjectives from Exercise 1.

1 Oh, no, we're _____! Come on. We'll miss the bus to school!
2 I'm so _____ about the concert tonight. Are you coming too?
3 Can you turn the music down please? It's very _____.
4 The science test was so _____. I think I need to study more.
5 I like my school because the teachers are so _____.
6 Oh, this bus is _____. Let's take the train next time – it's faster.
7 My friend thinks maths is _____, but I think it's very difficult.
8 My sister is a _____ swimmer. She wins all her swimming races!

◁)) 21 3 Listen to the conversation between Erin and Conrad. Who was at a party last night?

◁)) 21 4 Listen again. Tick (✓) the right sentence.

1 Erin isn't tired. ☐
  Conrad is tired. ☐
2 Erin was dancing. ☐
  Erin wasn't dancing. ☐
3 Conrad's brother's got a band. ☐
  Erin's brother's got a band. ☐
4 Conrad was at home. ☐
  Conrad wasn't at home. ☐
5 The dog wasn't loud. ☐
  The dog was loud. ☐

◁)) 21 5 Listen again. Write *Conrad* or *Erin*.

1 The party was for _____'s sister.
2 _____ loves dancing.
3 _____'s sister was happy.
4 _____ has got a test soon.
5 _____'s brother plays the guitar.
6 _____ was asleep at one o'clock.

GRAMMAR   Past simple: *be*

1 Choose the correct words.

1 I *was / were* tired after school.
2 My parents *was / were* very happy.
3 The history test *was / were* easy.
4 Where *was / were* you last night?
5 My friends *was / were* at the concert!
6 The birthday party was / were fun.
7 *Was / Were* you tired?
8 The film *was / were* brilliant.
9 My brother *was / were* late for the train.

2 Complete the conversation with *was* or *were*.

Leah: [1] .... the concert good, Oscar?
Oscar: Yes, it [2] ....! The musicians
[3] .... great.
Leah: [4] .... Lara there?
Oscar: Yes, she [5] .... She was very
excited.
Leah: And James?
Oscar: He [6] .... there too.
Leah: [7] .... you tired by the end of
the concert?
Oscar: Yes, we [8] ....! We
[9] .... home very late.

3 Write the negative form of the sentences.

1 My brothers were there.
....
2 We were tired.
....
3 I was bored.
....
4 It was cold.
....
5 It was dark.
....
6 My sisters were at a birthday party.
....
7 My friends were at a concert.
....
8 My parents were in the kitchen.
....
9 I was at home.
....

4 Complete the conversations with *was / wasn't* or *were / weren't*.

1 **A:** .... you and your family on the
beach yesterday?
B: No, we .... It ....
raining.

2 **A:** .... the food at the hotel good?
B: Yes, it .... The sandwiches
.... fantastic.

3 **A:** .... the rooms big?
B: No, they .... They
.... quite small.

4 **A:** .... there a swimming pool at
the hotel?
B: Yes, there ....
It .... big.

5 **A:** .... Charlie on holiday with you?
B: No, he .... He ....
at university.

6 **A:** .... you sad because of the
weather?
B: No, I .... I .... very
happy on my holiday.

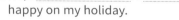

VOCABULARY AND READING

Adjectives (2)

1 Match the adjectives with the definitions.

1	quick	**a**	this describes a person's body, often their arms or legs
2	strong	**b**	this word describes something we enjoy, such as a party
3	fun	**c**	this is the opposite of 'old'
4	brilliant	**d**	this word means 'very good'
5	heavy	**e**	this word describes an object that weighs a lot and is difficult to carry
6	ready	**f**	this word is similar to 'happy'; we often say it when we meet a person for the first time
7	new	**g**	this is another word for 'fast'
8	pleased	**h**	we use this word to say we can start doing something

2 Complete the sentences with the adjectives from Exercise 1.

1 This is a very, very good film. It's _____!
2 You're so _____. I can't run that fast.
3 This is my _____ fitness tracker. I got it for my birthday.
4 My friend swims and plays tennis. She's very _____.
5 These bags are _____. Can you help me carry them, please?
6 Are you _____ to go, Jon? We've got to go now.
7 Everyone is enjoying Katie's party. We're having a _____ time.
8 Hello. I'm very _____ to meet you.

3 Read Henry's blog. Match the photos to the paragraphs.

1 _____ 2 _____ 3 _____ 4 _____

HENRY'S BLOG!

1 My name's Henry and this is my dad, Angus. Dad's got an interesting job: he takes photos of animals and he needs to travel a lot. In summer I always go with him.

2 We visit a different country every year! We always catch the train. It's more expensive than the bus, but I think it's more fun. At night, we sleep in our tent – it's great!

3 Our longest trip was to Turkey. We were there for three weeks. The weather wasn't great but there were some amazing buildings and the beaches were brilliant too! Some of my dad's photos were under water!

4 I always have a great time on our trips. I always put my tablet in my bag and I send emails and photos to my friends. My dad's bag is bigger than my bag. In his bag, there is always a small knife, a water bottle, our train tickets and, of course, his camera!

4 Read the blog again. Answer the questions.

1 How does Henry describe his dad's job?

2 What is Henry's dad's job?

3 When does Henry travel with his dad?

4 Do they always travel to the same country?

5 How do they travel: by bus or train?

6 How long was their trip to Turkey?

7 What was the weather like in Turkey?

8 What does Henry always put in his bag?

1 Match the verbs with their past simple ending.

1 help
2 phone
3 play
4 clean   **a** -ed
5 change
6 show   **b** -d
7 like
8 start   **c** -ied
9 study
10 close

2 Write the past simple of the verbs.

1 invite
2 live
3 love
4 walk
5 ask
6 want
7 work
8 open
9 carry

3 Complete the sentences with verbs from Exercise 2.

1 Milo usually cycles to school, but on Monday morning, he _____ to school with his sister.
2 After school on Wednesday, Paula and Marta were at a concert with their mother. They _____ it!
3 My mum _____ at a university before she became a teacher.
4 The science museum _____ at 9. Dad and I were the first ones there!
5 Sam _____ to go to the park yesterday, but it was too cold.
6 On Friday, my friend _____ me to her birthday party.
7 When Robbie was younger his grandparents _____ near his house, but now they live in a different city.
8 On Tuesday, Helena's maths teacher _____ her a difficult question.
9 My friend _____ my books for me because they were heavy.

4 Look at the pictures. Write sentences in the past simple. Use the verbs in the box.

clean	play	talk	walk

1 The children _____.

2 He _____.

3 She _____.

4 The children _____.

5 Complete the text. Use the verbs in the box in the past simple.

be	be	carry	clean
play	study	wash	watch

What a day! I'm *so* tired. This morning I ¹_____ my room. After that I ²_____ the car with my sister and my dad. It ³_____ so dirty!
In the afternoon, I ⁴_____ for next week's history test. When I finished studying, I ⁵_____ football in the garden. After that, it was time for dinner. I ⁶_____ hungry. I ⁷_____ the clean plates, knives and forks to the table.
In the evening, I ⁸_____ some music videos online and now it's time to go to sleep.

1 Look at the photos. Choose the correct words.

1 bird / kitten   2 rabbit / mouse   3 cow / donkey   4 mouse / sheep

5 dog / cat   6 sheep / rabbit   7 kitten / puppy   8 donkey / cow

2 Write the plural form.

1 dog
2 puppy
3 bird
4 cat
5 kitten
6 cow
7 donkey
8 sheep
9 rabbit
10 mouse

3 Write *F* for farm animal, *P* for pet or *B* for both.

1 rabbit		6 puppy	
2 mouse		7 cow	
3 bird		8 sheep	
4 dog		9 donkey	
5 kitten		10 cat	

4 🔊 22 Listen to the radio programme. What unusual pets has Logan got?

5 🔊 22 Listen again. Put the sentences in the order you hear them.

A Would you like to have other animals as pets?
B Have you got any other unusual pets?
C The mice sometimes come into the house.
D My first unusual pet was a snake.
E We'd like to have a zoo to help animals that are sick and need help.
F I'd love to have monkeys, crocodiles and elephants.
G We've got a kind of zoo for snakes.

1 Write the negative form of these verbs.

1 answer _____
2 lived _____
3 loved _____
4 started _____
5 wanted _____
6 worked _____
7 studied _____
8 walked _____
9 changed _____
10 cleaned _____
11 enjoyed _____

2 Match to make sentences.

1 Steven was tired and he didn't _____ b
2 The exam wasn't difficult and Jon _____
3 Rachel's pizza was too big. She didn't _____
4 Cory is 20 years old. He loves sport now but he didn't _____
5 Malcolm was a teacher. He didn't _____
6 Ian's homework wasn't easy. He didn't _____

a answered all the questions.
b want to play basketball.
c work in a hospital.
d eat it all.
e finish it until ten o'clock at night.
f like it when he was 11!

3 Write the negative form of the sentences.

1 My brother finished primary school in July.

2 I loved watching TV when I was a baby.

3 My friend started English lessons when she was three.

4 We enjoyed the birthday party at the weekend.

5 My sister walked to school yesterday.

6 I visited my grandparents on Sunday.

7 We started Spanish class in September.

8 My sister wanted to see the film.

9 I asked lots of questions at school last week.

1 Read the story. Put the underlined verbs into the past simple.

We [1]are on holiday in the Carpathian Mountains in Romania. Mum and Dad [2]don't like hotels — that is why we [3]are in a tent. It [4]is a bit cold at night, but we [5]enjoy staying in the tent. It [6]is Saturday — our last night of the holiday. Everyone in my family [7]is tired, but I [8]don't want to go to sleep. I [9]want to tell stories. We [10]are in our sleeping bags. Then there [11]is a noise. Everyone [12]listens. There [13]is the noise again! [14]Is it a bear? At that moment my sister [15]walks into the tent. 'Surprise!'

1 _____   6 _____   11 _____
2 _____   7 _____   12 _____
3 _____   8 _____   13 _____
4 _____   9 _____   14 _____
5 _____   10 _____   15 _____

2 Look at the photos. Complete the story with the words in the box.

door garden aunt house snake

My [1]_____ Alice phoned. She invited me to her [2]_____. She wanted to show me something. Alice lived near me. I walked there. She opened the [3]_____. 'Hello my dear. Come to the [4]_____.' There was a [5]_____ in the grass. I looked at it. It moved slowly. It was beautiful.

3 Tell your own animal story. Use past simple verbs.

_____
_____
_____
_____

Acknowledgements

The authors and publishers acknowledge the following sources of copyright material and are grateful for the permissions granted. While every effort has been made, it has not always been possible to identify the sources of all the material used, or to trace all copyright holders. If any omissions are brought to our notice, we will be happy to include the appropriate acknowledgements on reprinting and in the next update to the digital edition, as applicable.

Key: U = Unit, SU= Starter Unit.

Photography
The following images are sourced from Getty Images.

SU: ONOKY – Brooke Auchincloss/Brand X Pictures; Image Source; VikramRaghuvanshi/E+; ONOKY – Brooke Auchincloss/Brand X Pictures; American Images Inc/Photodisc; Rob Lewine; Westend61; U1: FatCamera/iStock/Getty Images Plus; Klaus Vedfelt/Riser; Caiaimage/Robert Daly; Ragnar Schmuck; EduLeite/E+; Westend61; Design Pics/Ron Nickel; Kane Skennar/DigitalVision; Steve Debenport/iStock/Getty Images Plus; Nancy Honey/Cultura; Nancy R. Cohen/Photodisc; U2: RubberBall Productions/Brand X Pictures; Fgorgun/E+; znur Kaya/EyeEm; gmtlu/E+; gmtlu/E+; Thomas Barwick/Stone; Thurtell/E+; Image Source; Glenn Gregory/EyeEm; U3: Steven Taylor/Photographer's Choice; Auris/iStock/Getty Images Plus; Eric Audras/ONOKY; nikkytok/iStock/Getty Images Plus; Halfdark; Spiderstock/E+; SolStock/iStock/Getty Images Plus; moodboard/Cultura; Johnce/E+ SolStock/E+; Steve Debenport/E+; Maskot; Tim Hall/Cultura; U4: Zoonar/homydesign/Getty Images Plus; Ulf Wittrock/EyeEm; EXTREME-PHOTOGRAPHER/iStock/Getty Images Plus; TORSTEN SILZ/DDP; David Franklin/Photographer's Choice RF; Hemera Technologies/PhotoObjects.net/Getty Images Plus; ULTRA.F/Photodisc; Busakorn Pongparnit/Moment; margouillatphotos/iStock/Getty Images Plus; Fred-D/iStock/Getty Images Plus; Fuse/Corbis; mkakade711@gmail.com/Moment; agalma/iStock/Getty Images Plus; Ilaria Baggio/EyeEm; Comstock Images/Stockbyte; kali9/iStock/Getty Images Plus; U5: Uwe Umstatter Tim Hughes/Lonely Planet Images; Rafa Fernndez/EyeEm; Tim Macpherson/Cultura Tetra Images; Sollina Images/Blend Images; Patrick Fraser/DigitalVision; Devonyu/iStock/Getty Images Plus; Jupiterimages/Stockbyte; UpperCut Images; Marc Leon/Cultura; VLIET/iStock Unreleased; petriartturiasikainen/E+; U6: Image Source; Wong Sze Fei/EyeEm; gmtlu/Stockbyte; Elenathewise/iStock/Getty Images Plus; Aleksandra Piss/Moment; Galiyah Assan/iStock/Getty Images Plus; Boarding1Now/iStock/Getty Images Plus; Richard Coombs/EyeEm; Pongasn68/iStock/Getty Images Plus; 10'000 Hours/DigitalVision; nito100/iStock/Getty Images Plus; U7: skynesher/E+; opreaistock/iStock/Getty Images Plus; Marc Romanelli/Blend Images; Image Source; SolStock/E+; nycshooter/E+; monkeybusinessimages/iStock/Getty Images Plus; Photodisc; Laurie and Charles/DigitalVision; Layland Masuda/Moment Open; Westend61; Wilfried Krecichwost/Stockbyte; U8: John Cumming/The Image Bank; Hero Images; Blend Images – JGI/Jamie Grill/Brand X Pictures; Martin Barraud/Caiaimage; Echo/Juice Images; Chris Ryan/OJO Images; U9: Tetra Images – Erik Isakson/Brand X Pictures; Jade/Blend Images; GoodLifeStudio/iStock/Getty Images Plus; Jose Luis Pelaez/Corbis/VCG; Dan Thornberg/EyeEm; Enes Evren/iStock/Getty Images Plus; Nickolai Vorobiov/EyeEm; Westend61; Thomas Northcut/Photodisc; mixetto/E+; Kisa_Markiza/iStock/Getty Images Plus; LWA/Larry Williams/Blend Images; Halfpoint/iStock/Getty Images Plus; Yuri_Arcurs/iStock/Getty Images Plus; Dave & Les Jacobs/Blend Images/Getty Images Plus; JGI/Jamie Grill/Blend Images; ferrantraite/E+; Ulrike Schmitt-Hartmann/Moment; KidStock/Blend Images; U10: Fabio Pagani/EyeEm; Dennie Cody and Duangkamon Khattiya/Photolibrary; AndreyKaderov/iStock/Getty Images Plus; Hill Street Studios/Blend Images; Belyaevskiy/iStock/Getty Images Plus; Juice Images; ClarkandCompany/E+; SolStock/iStock/Getty Images Plus; Nick Dolding/Cultura; Razvan Chisu/EyeEm; Jobalou/DigitalVision Vectors; Compassionate Eye; Foundation/Robert Kent/DigitalVision; ROMAOSLO/E+; fotokostic/ iStock/Getty Images Plus; shapecharge/E+; zoomphotographics/UpperCut Images; stereostok/iStock/Getty Images Plus; martin-dm/iStock/Getty Images Plus; Daisy-Daisy/iStock/Getty Images Plus; Igor Emmerich/Image Source; U11: Olaf Herschbach/EyeEm; Dorling Kindersley; ©fitopardo.com/Moment; Elke Meitzel/Cultura; Kevin Dodge/Corbis; Nophamon Yanyapong/EyeEm; stocknroll/iStock/Getty Images Plus; Juanmonino/

iStock/Getty Images Plus; Relax Images/Cultura; Michael Blann/Taxi; XiXinXing/iStock/Getty Images Plus; U12: Hero Images; Sal Alas/Moment; Fotonen/iStock/Getty Images Plus; Smneedham/Photolibrary; Jay's photo/Moment; Markus Guhl/Photodisc; milanfoto/E+; matty2x4/E+; RealisticFilm/iStock/Getty Images Plus; Jay's photo/Moment; AndrewScherbackov/iStock/Getty Images Plus; Jitalia17/iStock/Getty Images Plus; Korovin/iStock/Getty Images Plus; Bildverlag Bahnmuller/imageBROKER; Ronnie Kaufman/Larry Hirshowitz/Blend Images; U13: Steve Debenport/iStock/Getty Images Plus; Alan Brutenic/EyeEm; Freezingtime/iStock/Getty Images Plus; Spaces Images/Blend Images; zoranm/E+; Tom Werner/DigitalVision; Fuse/Corbis; Greg Kelner/EyeEm; Jetta Productions/Blend Images; bjdlzx/iStock/Getty Images Plus; JackF/iStock/Getty Images Plus; shomos uddin/Moment; Bertl123/iStock/Getty Images Plus; Alberto Manuel Urosa Toledano/Moment Open; VitalyEdush/iStock Editorial/Getty Images Plus; U14: den-belitsky/iStock/Getty Images Plus; kasto80/iStock/Getty Images Plus; Manakin/iStock/Getty Images Plus; Olha Romaniuk/iStock/Getty Images Plus; sharply_done/E+; Apriori1/iStock/Getty Images Plus; Christophe LEHENAFF/Photononstop; George-Standen/iStock Unreleased; Image Source; Henrik5000/iStock/Getty Images Plus; Alexander Spatari/Moment; Haykal/Moment; David Bank/Moment; UpperCut Images; U15: xavierarnau/E+; IMAGEMORE Co, Ltd.; MOAimage/Moment; C Squared Studios/Stockbyte; ronniechua/iStock/Getty Images Plus; lashah28/iStock/Getty Images Plus; ajr_images/iStock/Getty Images Plus; Avel Shah/EyeEm; Ljupco/iStock/Getty Images Plus; Westend61; Mieke Dalle/Photographer's Choice; Miguel Sanz/Moment; Kerkez/iStock/Getty Images Plus; Nick Dolding/DigitalVision; MartinPrescott/E+; Image Source; U16: vgajic/E+; ArtCookStudio/iStock/Getty Images Plus; Fuse/Corbis; Yulia-Kholodkova/iStock/Getty Images Plus; Richard Ransier/Corbis/VCG; Kirill Kukhmar/TASS; Tetra Images; U17: Photos by R A Kearton/Moment; Nick Brundle Photography/Moment; Glowimages; Julia Davila-Lampe/Moment; Nicolas Kipourax Paquet/Moment; earleliason/iStock/Getty Images Plus; Westend61; Daniel Alexander; L. Toshio Kishiyama/Moment; by Andrea Pucci/Moment; susandaniels/iStock/Getty Images Plus; Bonfanti Diego/Image Source; U18: dszc/iStock/Getty Images Plus; Pola Damonte via Getty Images/Moment; Jason Jones Travel Photography/Moment; www.bridgetdavey.com/Moment; DuKai photographer/Moment; ianwool/iStock/Getty Images Plus; Davide Seddio/Moment; U19: Design Pics; olesiabilkei/iStock/Getty Images Plus; vadimguzhva/iStock/Getty Images Plus; Halfpoint/iStock/Getty Images Plus; Simon Bottomley/Photographer's Choice RF; SerhiiBobyk/iStock/Getty Images Plus; Katja Kircher/Maskot; Chase Jarvis/DigitalVision; pchoui/E+; KenanOlgun/E+; valentinrussanov/iStock/Getty Images Plus; efesenko/iStock Editorial/Getty Images Plus; PhotoAlto/Eric Audras; U20: WestwindPhoto/iStock/Getty Images Plus; THEPALMER/E+; annick vanderschelden photography/Moment; Life On White/Stockbyte; Eric Dufour/EyeEm; guenterguni/E+; aaaaimages/Moment; Steve Debenport/E+; kate_sept2004/E+; Alex Potemkin/iStock/Getty Images Plus; urbancow/E+; © copyright kengoh8888/Moment; tiripero/iStock/Getty Images Plus; Roni Daya/iStock/Getty Images Plus; Photos by R A Kearton/Moment; Purple Collar Pet Photography/Moment ; Sergio Dilingua/EyeEm; Andy Roberts/Caiaimage; James Guilliam/EyeEm; Anna3571/iStock/Getty Images Plus; marydan15/iStock/Getty Images Plus; Hoxton/Tom Merton/ Hoxton; Akabei/iStock/Getty Images Plus; Kativ/iStock/Getty Images Plus.

The following photograph has been sourced from other library/ sources.

U7: Andrew Aitchison/Alamy Stock Photo.

Front cover photography by coldsnowstorm/iStock/Getty Images Plus/Getty Images.

Illustration
Amerigo Pinelli (Beehive Illustration Agency); Adz (Sylvie Poggio Artists Agency); Humberto Blanco (Sylvie Poggio Artists Agency); Amit Tayal (Sylvie Poggio Artists Agency); Nortbert Sipos (Beehive Illustration Agency); Simon Tegg; Mark Duffin.

The publishers are grateful to the following contributors: author of *Cambridge English Prepare! First Edition* Level 1 Workbook: Caroline Chapman; cover design and design concept: restless; typesetting: emc design Ltd; audio recordings: produced by Leon Chambers and recorded at The SoundHouse Studios, London; project management: Louise Davoren